MW00623787

Job Search Passport

Using Industry Secrets to Write Applications, Resumes and Cover Letters

The One Hour Handbook Series

by

Dr. Staci McIntosh

This is a work of nonfiction. Nonetheless, some of the names and personal characteristics of the individuals involved have been changed in order to disguise their identities. Any resulting resemblance to persons living or dead is entirely coincidental and unintentional.

Copyright © 2017 Staci McIntosh

All rights reserved. This book or any portion thereof may not be reproduced or used in any manner whatsoever without the express written permission of the publisher, except when appropriately cited and attributed to the author.

Published in the United States by Sensible Solutions
Henderson, Nevada

ISBN-13: 978-0-9992501-2-9
ISBN-10: 0-9992501-2-4

About the Author

S taci McIntosh has nearly 20 years of experience as a Human Resources executive in both public and private sectors. She has interviewed or coached over 1,000 individuals. Most have been just like you, wanting to perfect their skills for their next career move.

Staci writes her books with one goal: helping all people get the job they want. Through her brief, easy-to-read *One Hour Handbook Series,* she provides ambitious, hard-working people like you with useful tips you've probably never heard before. Staci knows her information will help you get your next job, because it's already worked for hundreds of others!

Staci entered the workforce as a teacher. She spent most of her career in the education field, eventually becoming an assistant superintendent and Chief Human Resources Officer. She then moved to the private sector. She is currently the Vice President of Human Resources for a popular casino resort on the Las Vegas Strip. Staci has a Bachelor's degree from Eastern Washington University, a Master's degree from Whitworth University, and an educational doctorate in leadership from Washington State University.

Staci lives with her husband Jim in Henderson, Nevada. Together they own Sensible Solutions, a consulting company devoted to providing practical resources for busy organizations and people. They enjoy eating great food on the Strip, binge-watching TV series, traveling, and spending time with Jim's teenage son Ben (an expert level Xbox One player) and Staci's daughter Kendall (a busy human resources professional).

To Mom and Dad

Table of Contents

Introduction

When I was an English teacher, all the seniors turned in their term papers in April. Consequently, all of the English teachers had dozens of long essays to read, each taking at least fifteen to twenty minutes. We used to joke to the students that the way we really graded their papers was to throw the piles down a flight of stairs. Whichever papers reached the bottom would get A's, those which only made it half-way down got C's, and so on.

Sometimes the hard work you do to submit paperwork to employers feels like that. A waste of time. Futile. Useless. Even if you've completed applications before, processes change. The era of online applications, e-signatures, and resume uploads creates more confusion and less transparency. This book will help you navigate a successful journey. Maybe you're a savvy job search guru, but you just need some additional tweaks to update your approach. Maybe you're completely new to the job market. Maybe you're a recent college graduate. Maybe you were just fired. Maybe you're entering the job search process after being a stay at home parent. Maybe you're a retiree returning to work.

Whatever your current employment status, you might be wondering, why do I have to answer all of those questions? How does this whole online thing work? How do I know anyone even got my application? Why haven't I heard from human resources? Why does it take so long to get a response? Does a cover letter matter anymore? Who sees my resume? Why can't I just hand them a paper application?

If you have questions like this, you've chosen the right book! I'm going to answer those questions. I'm first going to give you strategies to use when preparing your paperwork. You will choose the right strategy based on your specific situation. Then I'm going to give you technical details about the process and specific guidance for the content and wording you should use to complete each and every portion.

If you're stuck and frustrated, you'll find all sorts of tips and tricks to forge ahead. Using my years of human resources experience in both the public and private sector, I will give you insight you won't see as an applicant. Your efficiency and productivity will increase, and your frustration will decrease. Most importantly, after following my advice, you will begin to get plenty of interviews.

In Chapter One, I tell you the strategies you will use to approach your job search, depending on why you're looking for a job. In Chapter Two, I will explain how to network in order to maximize your job possibilities. Chapter Three discloses what happens to your job search paperwork once you submit it to the employer. If you bought this book at midnight because you're lost and in the middle of an online application, focus on Chapters Four, Five, Six and Seven. In those chapters you will find specific information, tips and tricks for completing the online application, writing the cover letter and developing a resume. Chapter Four tells you how to complete each section of the application itself. Chapter Five shows you how to adapt your resume to different job postings and industries. Chapter Six explains the essential components of a cover letter. Chapter Seven gives you a list of common mistakes to avoid.

Finally, in Chapter Eight, I share possible barriers if you aren't getting an interview, and how to overcome them. In any chapter, jump to the "Take the Shortcut" section to get a short summary. This is particularly useful if you're on a deadline and only have time to consider the most important info. Whatever you need, you're going to find it in this book. And if you don't find it here, email me at stacimcintosh23@gmail.com. I will be happy to answer your questions, because it will help me add what readers need to future updates!

Chapter One

Why Are You Looking?

Guess what? No matter why you're looking for a job, after reading this book, you will experience success. If you're a recent college graduate, you're probably saying, *Well duh, I rock! Of course I'll find a job.* Rightfully so. You just finished a college degree. Congratulations! You do rock!

If you're returning to work after a long absence, or if you were fired, you feel quite differently. You've probably thought of plenty reasons why you won't get hired. Too old. Too outdated. Too dumb. Too damaged. Too screwed over by your former employer. Too this, or too that.

In the job search process, your success is not primarily determined based on your circumstances. Instead, your success is much more about about the perception of your future employer. If you think you are awesome, that's great, but you'd better make sure the future employer perceives you are a match for that specific job. If you think you suck or if you think your previous employer sucked, you must use strategies to make sure your future employer doesn't see it that way.

The good news is that you can easily influence how your future employer perceives your job search. You do this by simply ensuring that the approach you use varies, depending on your situation. For each common job search circumstance, I will provide you with the specific strategies you need to influence perception.

Go to the section that applies to you. After reading it, you will understand how to approach your paperwork. I will explain how recruiters and hiring managers perceive you as an applicant. I will also explain how you should *want* them to perceive you. In addition, I give you specific phrases, words, and explanations to use throughout your paperwork. Finally, in each section, I will provide cautions regarding what *not* to do in your situation.

I'm New to the Job Market

If you are new to the job market, you have special job search status. This is the only time you'll have that special status. Enjoy it while it lasts! Strategically, you'll want to leverage your special-ness at every point in the process. This is true whether you are seeking a job in high school or if you are a college graduate.

You will generally be perceived as a hot new prospect. Your first goal is to take it up a notch. You want to be perceived as a hot new prospect who is desired by multiple employers and who has many employment options. You want to make it seem like a seller's market. You're selling *you,* and there are plenty of buyers.

In order to foster that perception, keep your search focused. Don't apply to a great many positions with the same company. Two or three in the same job category is about the maximum. Make it appear that you are more particular than you really are. Above all else, you don't want to seem desperate. You want employers to see you as picky, thoughtful and strategic in your job search.

Your second goal is to minimize your lack of formal work experience. Do so by maximizing the skills and traits you do have. Read the job posting carefully. Using your resume and cover letter, highlight your characteristics that match the desired experiences and traits listed on the posting.

Your third goal is to show your work ethic and commitment. Include all of the experiences you gained outside your role as a student. Examples are your participation on athletic teams, your work volunteering, and your leadership of special projects or committees. This will also include any internships or short-term jobs that apply to the position you want. Try to show that during your time in school, you acquired increased levels of knowledge, experience, and responsibility.

If you have been unable to obtain a career-track job after graduating from college several months prior, avoid making your job search difficulty obvious. Instead, tell employers that you chose to travel, or *wanted* to experience other work roles, before settling in to your career dream job. Generally speaking, you will not have to worry about a perception issue if you handle it correctly. Many college graduates choose to pursue other interests before settling down. Give the impression that was the case for you, and there will be an automatic assumption that you are employable.

The bottom line: Make them perceive you as picky, valuable, and highly sought after. Don't look desperate.

I'm Ready for a Promotion

If you're applying because you want a promotion, you have the most enviable status. You don't need a job. You just want a promotion. It is always better to have a job when you are looking for a job. Future employers know that another organization already vetted you. Another employer hired you and found you worthy to keep around. Therefore, the future employer thinks, you must be good.

Whenever you are employed while searching, it's automatically a seller's market. You're the seller of you. They're the buyer. If you are in this enviable position, future employers know you could be hired by anyone. Your first goal is therefore to have them perceive you as an extremely desirable, and competitive, candidate. You want them to believe you are highly likely to get multiple job offers. This makes them more likely to interview you.

Your second goal in this situation should be to enhance the perception of you as a high-achieving, super star employee. Do this by focusing on the traits and skills the job requires. When preparing your resume and cover letter, highlight how your skills and experiences match those requirements.

A third goal is to make the hiring manager believe that the job you want is the next logical step on a quickly rising career ladder. Do this by ensuring the job experiences on your resume show an increasing level of responsibility, even if the position title was the same throughout. On the application, when it asks why you left that position, state clearly, *I was promoted to a position with a higher level of responsibility*. Be sure to list all the positions you had with that same employer in order to show how promotable you have been.

Sometimes it happens that people been employed by one organization for several years. When they seek a promotion, that organization declines to promote them numerous times. If that situation applies to you, your approach will be slightly different.

Your first goal in that case is to broaden your job search to other companies. Don't be afraid of switching employers. Moving across companies and organizations is one of the fastest ways to get promoted. This is because many people don't like change. Others are place bound and cannot move geographic locations in order to get a promotion. If you can, be open to the possibility of a geographic move. That will exponentially maximize your opportunities.

Your second goal is to emphasize how much you have learned in the role you've had. Focus your written information accordingly. Make it look as if you were a promotable employee, even if your job title didn't change. Emphasize that you were gaining additional responsibilities and experience.

In both situations, never disclose how many jobs you have applied for. You will appear desperate for a promotion. That will make you less desirable as a candidate. Remember, you want to foster the perception that you have multiple job options. And you want to make yourself seem picky.

In order to do that, wait as long as it takes for the right opportunity to present itself. Keep your search focused. Don't apply to a great many positions with the same company. Choosing just one is ideal. Two is the maximum. Three will make you seem desperate.

When my husband Jim switched organizations, he wasn't even looking for a new position. The new employer considered it desirable that Jim hadn't applied anywhere else. They felt it showed Jim's commitment that theirs was one of the few jobs Jim would have considered.

When my daughter graduated and went to college, I knew I wanted to move to Las Vegas. My future employer found it desirable that I was choosing to move. I didn't need a job. I only wanted a challenging opportunity in a new city.

Again, you are in a highly desirable situation. You can afford to be choosey. You can afford to wait until the right opportunity presents itself. When it does, future employers will feel like they've found a needle in a haystack, because they will perceive that you only considered a few promotional opportunities.

The bottom line: Make yourself seem desirable and patient rather than desperate for a promotion.

I Was a Stay-At-Home Parent

If you were able to stay at home while raising your children, count yourself lucky! These days it's very difficult to afford a one-income family.

It is extremely common for stay-at-home parents to return to work when their children make a school transition. There is no reason to be discouraged because you haven't worked in a while. It's true that some employers might perceive your skills as outdated. However, your chances will improve dramatically by making a few adaptations to your job search strategy.

The most important goal when you are returning to work after a lengthy parenting stint is for future employers to perceive you as a lucky find. You want them to see you as a candidate who brings varied and current skills to the role. You want them to see you as a motivated, hard worker who is excited to get back into the job market. You want them to perceive you as so valuable that they don't really pay attention to the fact that you've been at home for a few years. How you achieve this goal will be dependent on the length and type of experience you had prior to staying home with the kids.

If you had only entry-level experience when you left the job market, highlight your experience parenting and managing the household. List your specific skills in your resume and reference them in the cover letter to show how they help you meet the job expectations. Ideally, part of your experience includes volunteer work where you managed projects or events and had to work well with others. That type of experience translates well into many entry-level positions.

If you had extensive professional-level experience prior to your decision to stay home with kids, you need to show that you have remained current in your line of work. Prior to returning to full-time work, begin temporary work in your professional area and do some consulting. Attend continuing education or seminars. Reference these recent experiences when preparing your resume and your cover letter in order to show your skills are current.

If you don't have recent consulting or other temporary work, highlight the skills you do have. Get recent experience while you're looking for a job.

In your cover letter, give examples from your prior work history and then add how or why it's still relevant today. Make it explicit that you've continued learning while home, and that you can now reflect even more wisely upon your past experiences.

Your second goal in both circumstances is to ensure future employers know you are excited to be working again. You want employers to see you as someone who is motivated, not someone who had nothing better to do than go back to work. In your cover letter, be sure to discuss how enthusiastic you are to begin contributing to the overall success of an organization. Mention the satisfaction you will feel helping others outside of your immediate family.

Your third goal is to minimize hiring managers' focus on the time you spent at home. You can do this by elaborating on your skills while barely mentioning your recent stay-at-home parenting role. You want hiring managers to read a lot about all the wonderful traits you will bring to the job. If you elaborate on your skills well, hiring managers will focus on that information while not thinking much about your time at home. Hiring managers want the very best person for the job. If you can help them overlook the fact that you don't have recent experience, they will see you as a competitive candidate.

In your paperwork, refrain from details about the specific reason why you're returning to work. Avoid saying anything about money. Don't explain that now you need a steady paycheck because your kids were admitted to an expensive college. Don't mention you got divorced and now you need to work full-time. Your only reason for returning to work should be that you are excited to contribute to a large organization again. If anything, you can add that you are fortunate your kids are now ready to be more independent.

In addition, don't provide overly specific personal details unless they are related to the job posting. For example, you generally wouldn't explain that the reason you stayed home was because one of your children had special needs. However, if you are applying for a teacher's aide position in a special education classroom, that detail would be pertinent. Focus on the skills you have to contribute to the employer's success. That's what the employer is interested in.

The bottom line: Elaborate on your knowledge, skills and applicable experience while minimizing information about your time at home.

I'm an Older and Wiser Retiree

If you retired after a long career and now want or need to return to work, you can quite easily do so. It's true that some employers might not realize you're as fabulous as you are. However, most will value the maturity and skills you bring to the table.

This is even more true if you're looking for part-time work. The reason is that many people can't afford to work only part time. This makes it difficult for employers. Basically, it's you, the teenagers, and the twenty-somethings who haven't yet found a career. Adhere to some important strategies and you will have a job in no time.

The most important goal when you are returning to work as a retiree is to create the perception that you're a bored retiree who yearns to work again. You want them to see you as a fortunate find and a mature, reliable team member, especially relative to your younger counterparts. Create this perception by developing a cover letter that emphasizes your enthusiasm for working again. In your resume, write about your broad skills more than your job-specific knowledge. This will allow you to access a diverse set of job types.

Your second goal is to have future employers see you as energetic and fun. You want them to believe you are someone who will bring a mature yet easy-going demeanor to the workplace. Strive to give the impression that you will fit in with the younger crowd without being influenced by their shenanigans.

Your third goal is to be less specific in your job search than you might have been during your career. Consider multiple ways to earn money. If you were a professional, you could return to work on a per-hour basis as a contractor or temporary worker. For example, if you worked as an accountant, you could offer to fill in at companies who have temporary vacancies while look to hire someone permanently. If you want to explore multiple cities, sign up for an agency that places temporary professionals in longer-term positions for three months or more. You can experience different cities while earning extra money.

If you have skills that might meet a broad range of employer needs, apply to a temporary agency. They may not consistently have temp jobs that were in your line of work. However, they will have many others. Most temp agencies will allow you to indicate preferences for the days of week you want to work (or not) and your preferred hours (within reason).

Never state you need to return to work for the money. When you write your cover letter and resume, focus only on your enthusiasm for contributing to their organization's success. If employers believe you have only reluctantly returned to work, they will think you are bitter. They will envision you doing the work, but with a poor attitude. Combat that perception by making sure your cover letter is upbeat and positive. Feel free to poke a little fun at why you want to return to work during at this time in your life.

Finally, before you do anything, be sure to update your technology skills. If you have an AOL email account, get something more current. Nothing screams *I'm outdated* more than an AOL email account. Outlook, hotmail, and gmail are all free and easily created. If you don't know the basics of using Word, creating .pdf files, and saving documents on your computer, you can find free online classes on the internet. Go to www.edx.org or www.coursera.org to find what you need.

The bottom line: Cultivate the perception that you're an enthusiastic, mature contributor and not a bitter retiree forced to return to work.

I'm a Laid Off Top Performer

If you've been laid off, I'm sure it's stressful, but don't spend any time worrying! Your lay-off won't inhibit your job search. Remain positive and upbeat, adhere to some simple strategies, and you'll be fine.

Your goal after being laid off is to create the perception that you are, nevertheless, a very competitive candidate. You want hiring managers to see your involuntary job loss as an opportunity for them. By hiring you, they are getting a better candidate than they might normally be able to recruit from

13

another competitor.

To enhance that perception, emphasize your career at the previous company if it included frequent promotions, additional job responsibilities or special projects. Your paperwork should reflect strong successes. This will make it clear to the hiring manager that your job loss is their fortunate gain.

Your second goal is to make it clear you were laid off as part of a company-wide reduction. If you are among a small group of individuals being let go, the future employer might wonder if your layoff was actually due to lackluster performance. In that situation, it's even more important to provide details that clarify the reason for the layoff. If your company's lay off was commonly known in the community, you can usually avoid going into greater detail. This is because employers can easily verify the reason for the layoff on their own.

Another way to help make the layoff clear is to use full, explanatory sentences. Instead of writing *laid off* when the application asks you why you left, write it in sentence form. Examples are: *I was laid off due to company downsizing; My position was eliminated due to lack of revenue in the Asia division; I was laid off due to the company outsourcing the technology department.*

Finally be sure to list references on your resume. The references should include the names and phone numbers of your previous supervisors. The hiring manager won't call your supervisors unless you become a finalist. However, listing your supervisors from the company where you were laid off solidifies the impression that you were a top performer.

If you are not yet unemployed, there is no reason to disclose that you are about to be laid off. You can honestly write, *I am still employed* when the application asks for your reason for leaving the company. Focus instead on your desire for a new opportunity to contribute toward the success of a larger (or smaller) organization. Later, in the interview, you can mention you are aware lay-offs are likely in the future.

Also avoid any judgments or value statements about your former employer. Make it clear in your cover letter that you valued your tenure with them and loved working for them. Give the impression that you completely understand the reason for the layoffs, even if you don't.

The bottom line: Make it clear your lay-off was not related to your performance, and maintain a positive tone throughout your paperwork.

I Had to Move Cities

If the reason you are looking for a new job is that you have to move cities, you are in a good position. You haven't been let go, so there is no reason to explain your previous job loss.

Staying employed in your previous city for as long as possible will be to your advantage. By all means, do so if you are able. This shows future employers that your previous employer wants to keep you. On the application, you can indicate that you haven't left yet. Your desire to relocate will be in the cover letter, where you will give more information about your geographic move.

Your first goal is to help hiring managers perceive your geographic move as an opportunity for them. They are getting a better candidate than they might normally be able to find, and without the recruiting costs. You are already committed to moving, so they don't have to convince you to do so.

To ensure hiring managers see you as highly competitive, be sure you highlight your skills and experiences that match the job description. In your cover letter, include the information that you are seeking a geographic move to that city.

Your second goal is to ensure hiring managers know you are excited for the new challenge. You want them to believe you would want to work there even if you weren't moving. No one wants a candidate who is begrudgingly moving. Ensure they perceive you as upbeat and positive.

Your third goal is for future employers to see you as picky in your job search. If they view you as applying everywhere, you run the risk of being perceived as desperate. Give the perception that you are selectively applying only to a few companies that really interest you. In that way, you enhance the perception that you are a highly sought after candidate. When employers believe you don't need to work, or that you are waiting for the perfect job, they know they need to pursue you. This usually results in higher salary offers than you would get if they thought you were desperate for a job.

The level of detail you provide about your relocation depends on the reason itself. If you are a trailing spouse, you are safe explaining that in the cover letter. Just be sure to remain positive and frame it as an opportunity, rather than a burden.

If the reason for the move is to take care of a sick parent, or to be closer to your grandchildren, don't give that level of detail. Your future employer might see you as someone who's not that committed to work. Hiring managers might believe you'll be an employee who takes a lot of time off work for your family.

Instead, frame the move as serving two purposes. Tell them you want to move to be closer to your family *and* that you are ready for a new work challenge at an exciting company. If you haven't moved yet, give them the perception that you are waiting for the right job opportunity before moving. This gives the appearance that you are focused on finding the right challenge first, before your move.

The bottom line: Make employers see your move as lucky for them. Focus on your excitement about a new challenge. Make them see your move as more of a choice than a requirement.

I Was Fired for Not Meeting Performance Targets

Hey, it happens. You thought you were great at your job. Turns out, you weren't that fabulous. Or maybe you *were* fabulous, and your employer didn't realize it. Their loss. Don't worry. Follow my advice, and you'll have the chance to be fabulous at another job.

Before you even start applying, contact your former employer. If they didn't offer to let you quit instead of being fired, ask if they will allow you to resign instead. In exchange, you may be asked to sign an agreement stating that you won't sue them. Do it. If you were a union member, sometimes your union can help negotiate a resignation agreement as well. It's in your best interest to have a resignation instead of a termination.

Also find out what the employer will say if someone calls them for a reference check. If you know your boss really liked you, even though you weren't a fit for the job, that's a great situation to be in. You know you'll get a good reference on the skills you do have. If not, then the agreement should say that your former employer will only verify your employment and will *not* provide a reference.

17

In this situation, your most important goal is to convince hiring managers that you are a quality candidate. You want them to think that *you* made the decision to leave when *you* determined that the job wasn't working out. You want your paperwork to reflect only positive experiences, so you can get an interview. You want them to think *their* company will be a better match for your skills. Then, when they fall in love with you, they will overlook your less-than-ideal previous job situation.

Do this by carefully choosing how to explain why you left. Tell the truth, but frame your job loss in the most positive way possible. Choose thoughtfully what to emphasize and what to de-emphasize.

Avoid any mention of conflicts with your boss, the ridiculous work load, or the toxic competitive environment. If you choose your words incorrectly, you could be perceived as having a negative attitude about your former employer. Your potential employer will immediately be concerned that you may not be a quality candidate.

Instead, go out of your way to compliment the previous company regardless of what you thought about them. Emphasize the skills you have that the future employer wants. Focus your brain on your future happiness when you are writing the cover letter or the reason for your departure. By thinking positively about the future as you write, your optimism will be evident in your sentences. All of this will help enhance the impression that you are the one who decided to leave.

If you want to stay in the same field, another goal is to convince the future employer that there was something different about your previous work situation, something that won't apply to the future employer. For example, for a sales job, you might say, *I realized it would always be difficult to meet their sales quotas because I wasn't passionate about their product.* For a teaching job, you might say, *I realized that I felt too anonymous working in a large urban school district. That's why I want to work in a small school district now.* A waitress could say, *I loved the people I worked with, but there was some inconsistency in the food quality, so I had to handle several angry customers. I want to work in a restaurant where I can always be proud of the food I'm serving.*

Some individuals stay within the same career path, switch companies, then are fired from the new company. If you left the original organization in good standing, you can always recover from this situation. Employers know that company cultures and expectations are different. It's not unusual for a person to be successful in one organization and still not work out in another organization. It happens all the time, so don't be discouraged at all. It was a bad experience you can easily get over. Mention your surprise at how different the culture was at the company who fired you, and emphasize how valued you were at your original company.

If you're willing to change professions, you can overcome any negative perception even more easily. Most employers won't worry very much about you losing that sales position if it's not another sales job you want. You may have been a bad science teacher, but that doesn't mean you'll be a bad lab technician. You may have been a terrible waitress, but that doesn't mean you will be a terrible receptionist.

If you were new in a position and simply couldn't do the job you thought you could do, this is also quite easy to overcome. For the sales job, you could say, *I work great with people and have a strong work ethic. What I discovered is that I disliked being turned down by people who didn't want to buy the product. I think I probably needed to have a thicker skin to be in that type of high-pressure sales situation.* The teacher could write, *I always thought I wanted to be a teacher, but after my first year, I discovered that I didn't enjoy working with teenagers every day. I like kids, but I realized my preference is to have a career working with adults.* The waitress could say, *What I discovered is that being a waitress is a lot more difficult that it looks. I'm a fast worker, but when it was really busy, even I wasn't that fast!*

These employment situations are even less of a problem if you are newly out of college. Everyone knows that college degrees don't always translate to a successful career launch. If you are still in your twenties, it is even more understandable from an employer's point of view. If you were let go after you were only in that profession for a relatively short amount of time (about five years or less), you can easily explain it in a way that appears less negative. Employers understand that sometimes new career paths don't work out.

For all of the situations, in the language you use, give the impression that your departure was a mutual decision. You can state, *My supervisor and I agreed that I was unable to meet the targeted performance expectations, and I separated from the company under good conditions.* Note that this phrase simply leaves out information regarding who made the final decision for you to leave, if in fact it was not you.

In your cover letter, write that you are excited to be looking for a new challenge. State you want a position that is more aligned to your work habits, skills, and preferences. It is fine to use the cover letter to explain why your current career path was not appealing to you. Just be sure to focus on the type of work itself rather than the employer or your unreasonable supervisor.

Adapt the phrases I've suggested to your specific situation. Overall, strive for your paperwork to give the impression you are upbeat about your job search, optimistic about your future, and confident about your skills. All of that will add to the impression that there was nothing bad about your job loss, and you have nothing to hide.

It goes without saying that when you use positive sentences, you have to believe them. If you have to, spend reflection time coming to terms with your job loss. In other words, suck it up, get a grip, and move on with enthusiasm! If you are still angry or vengeful regarding how you were treated by your former employer, you won't be able to sound positive when explaining your job loss.

It really does help if you take time to meditate on, pray about, or talk through your feelings. Understand the situation from your former employer's point of view so that you can think positively about your future. My upcoming book *Brace For Landing: Rebooting Your Career After Being Laid Off, Pushed Out, Fired or Demoted* will provide more details about this process. It will help you come to terms with your involuntary job loss. In the meantime, if you want additional tips about how to wrangle your emotions into a more positive viewpoint, feel free to email me at stacimcintosh23@gmail.com.

The bottom line: Give the impression you are happy about changing jobs and you are excited for a new challenge.

I Was Fired for Doing Something Pretty Bad

So, you did something pretty bad, huh? Or, you got fired for doing something pretty bad, but you didn't do it? When they started to investigate, you left because you were afraid they'd find all the other things you actually did do? It was a witch hunt and you were on the losing end? You were afraid of the impact it would have on your family? Or, you had a really serious brain malfunction?

Listen, these things happen more than you think. Really good people, really smart people, really successful people, get fired for things that look pretty bad to the outside observer. In human resources terms, that's what we call misconduct.

The first thing to do is get strategic. Always attempt to negotiate a resignation agreement if you think there is any chance your employer can prove misconduct. When doing so, ensure that your employer will agree not to provide any reference at all should a future employer call. If you must, it's worth it to hire an attorney to negotiate with your human resources department. Your attorney can also help determine what leverage you can use to negotiate a better exit deal.

There's a really broad range of misconduct. When you begin to apply for jobs, it will be easier if yours is not as serious as some others. In these situations, the overarching goal in all of your paperwork is to give the impression that you resigned for a legitimate reason a future employer shouldn't be worried about. You want to make it seem like *you* wanted to switch jobs. You want the future employer to believe you're excited about a new opportunity.

Another goal is to be vague, yet truthful, during the paperwork process. You are better off if your future employer believes you were terminated for poor performance than for misconduct. Based on your paperwork, the hiring manager might assume this is the case. That is to your advantage, and showing you are confident and excited about your job search (even if you aren't) will enhance the perception.

There are some situations that will make it easier for you to give the impression nothing bad happened. One is if your employer had an initial belief you did something wrong, but you resigned before anything was proven. Another is if the allegation was bad, but no one knew about the misconduct except your direct supervisor and human resources, you went away quietly, and they agreed to confidentiality. Another is if you weren't arrested and it didn't make the local news. If you were allowed to give your coworkers a plausible reason for your departure, that will be the reason that sticks. Another improved situation for you is if your employer has a vested interest in not letting the public know why you really left, because it would make them look bad if their investors or other individuals with powerful interests found out.

On the other hand, your job search will unfortunately be harder if the circumstances surrounding your firing involved any of the following: a crime for which you were charged; a well-known or media-publicized event; an employer who refused a confidentiality agreement; or, any situation where you know your future employer will hear details about your firing. Note that I said your job search would be *harder*. But it is definitely *possible* to work again. So, if you screwed up or if you were screwed over, take heart. There is a pathway to job success again!

Another goal in this situation is to give a future employer the impression that whatever you did was the unfortunate outcome of a temporary situation or condition. And, it must be a situation or condition that you can say has been diagnosed, addressed, or resolved.

Consider if your misconduct was related to any of the following conditions:

1. *You had an addiction.* Your gambling addiction may have caused you to embezzle money. Your drug addiction may have caused you to steal. Your alcohol addiction may have caused you to arrive drunk on the job. Your sex addiction may have caused you to sexually harass others or engage in sexual misconduct on the job.

2. *You had a diagnosable psychiatric illness.* If you were clinically depressed, you may have demonstrated attendance issues. Any number of mental illnesses may have caused you to steal products, scream at your boss, lose your temper with your coworkers, or behave in a sexually inappropriate manner.

3. *You were in a temporary life situation that negatively impacted your judgment.* People who are having a crisis in their personal life can make bad choices. Those bad choices can be made out of fear, depression, grief, anger or a general feeling of not being valued, heard, or recognized. For example, perhaps you had a health situation. It may have caused you to go into deep debt, causing you to fear losing your house, which caused you to embezzle money. Maybe your spouse left you for another person and you began sexting younger coworkers, drinking too much, or creating conflicts with everyone at work who reminded you of your spouse.

All of these situations are unfortunate if you know that future employers will be made aware of what occurred. However, if you show that you took steps to fix the situation, many employers will give you a second chance. This assumes three conditions: 1) you took responsibility for the situation on the application; 2) your previous employer gives the same reason for your termination as you do, or ideally, will only provide your work history, and; 3) you openly share that you have learned from your mistake and you specify what steps you took to address the issue such as receiving treatment, completing therapy, or paying restitution.

That said, only be up front if you are certain your former employer will eventually say exactly why you were fired. And, you don't need to write too much unless asked to provide specific details. When you initially write about the situation, try to avoid full disclosure. Don't directly give the reason for your termination, if you can avoid doing so. It is acceptable for you to write a truthful but vague answer.

You need not make it obvious what occurred. If asked for the reason you left your position, you might write, *I was in a difficult situation that impacted my work. Ultimately, my employer and I parted ways, and I fully understood their position. The situation has since been resolved.* This answer is truthful without causing the hiring manager to automatically disqualify your application.

Your hope is that you can get to the interview. There, hopefully your past will be overshadowed by your outstanding answers to the interview questions. In the cover letter, you need not refer to the misconduct at all. Focus on the skills you bring to the new position and your excitement and passion for a new challenge. Your goal is to stay truthful without calling attention to the fact that you were terminated for misconduct.

If, later in the process, the future employer asks for more details, anything other than honesty is going to cause them to dig deeper into your background. When asked to provide more details, give simple, short answers. Address the situation enough so they don't feel the need to obtain even more information.

It is a delicate balance. You must give them enough details so they can understand the situation in general. But you don't want to give too many details. Otherwise, they may doubt you've been rehabilitated.

Another important goal is to be optimistic, yet realistic. If you've been looking for a while without success, you might want to rethink your expectations about your next job. It may take some time to find another job within the same line of work and/or at the same level as your previous position. Consider taking a job with a little less pay or responsibility in order to prove yourself. Then begin moving up the ladder again.

Although it may be hard to do, it's also important that you maintain a positive mindset. This will help keep you motivated to fill out applications. It will ensure you have the confidence to pursue the work you love. Most importantly, it will help you project an image of an energetic, collaborative potential employee. You need to really believe your mistake is just that:

only a mistake. It doesn't define who you are. It is only a set of bad circumstances that you can decide to overcome.

When you've been fired for misconduct, it's also extremely important you stay busy during the job search. This will help you meet more people who will develop trust in you. Ideally, you may be able to work for a temporary placement agency. If, because of your termination, you cannot be a temp within your previous line of work, try a different type of work. When you work for a temp agency, you meet a variety of employers who will get to know you. This can help you get hired permanently.

Volunteer work is also an option if you are unable to obtain even temporary employment. Choose volunteer activities where you will have the opportunity to meet as many people as possible. Treat your volunteer work like a job. Eventually people will notice you, and you may be able to get referrals to paying jobs.

Hopefully, your only work issue was the one-time misconduct you were accused of. Your advanced skills will eventually become apparent to your new employer. You will start moving up the ladder again, even if you had to go down a few steps in order to do so.

The bottom line: Be vague in your statements while demonstrating a positive outlook in all of your paperwork. Only give details if you have to. Seek temporary or volunteer work to prove yourself.

Take the Shortcut

1. The reason why you are looking for a job should determine how you approach your job search.

2. Your goal in all situations is to submit paperwork that is positive, upbeat, and gives the impression that you left your previous employer under the best circumstances possible.

3. Highlight the experiences and skills you have which match those listed on the position description.

4. Always speak well of your former employer, and always give the impression you are excited to be pursuing a new job challenge.

5. If you lost your job because you were fired for not meeting job expectations, your goal is to make it apparent in your paperwork that, although your skills may not have matched your previous job, you would be a valuable employee in a different type of job.

6. If you lost your job due to misconduct, your goal is to submit paperwork that is truthful yet vague enough for the future employer to still consider giving you an interview.

7. Because all situations are unique, use the information in this chapter as a guide in preparing your paperwork. Depending on your specific circumstances, you may need to adapt your approach to better fit the situation. Email me at stacimcintosh23@gmail.com if you have a question about your specific job search.

Chapter Two

Being in the Right Place at the Right Time

I'm sure at some point in your life, you knew someone who landed a great job. You may have said to yourself, *That person was just lucky. He was in the right place at the right time!* I know I've thought that before. I've known people who left one job under really bad circumstances and still received multiple job offers right away. I thought geez, that person is so lucky!

Want to know how they did it? Yes, you do. It's really quite simple. Follow the advice in this chapter, and you'll find yourself in the right place, at the right time, to get the right job.

One reason this happens is what you probably already know. Someone knows someone who knows someone. Ultimately, the candidate's name gets referred to the person at the other end of the paperwork trail. That's important because so many people usually apply to one position.

More specifically, the use of online applications makes it easy for multitudes of individuals to apply for any one job. It doesn't mean all the applications will be high quality. It does mean that hiring managers will use any information they can to narrow the pool of candidates. Receiving positive information about a candidate, regardless of the content, helps hiring managers identify those they will interview.

Completing application paperwork using the right words, the right tone, and the right level of detail is important. However, knowing the people who may be looking at your application is ideal. I'm going to teach you how to leverage your connections to help you in this way.

Of course, networking is critical. Yes it's hard for some people. And it can be intimidating. And time consuming. But you will learn tips for doing it in this chapter. I will explain how you can leverage the networking web to your advantage. I will describe how to network through your professional contacts, whether or not you still have a job. I will describe how to utilize community resources to show others your value and get referrals. Finally, I will describe how to use social media to maximize your networking opportunities.

The Networking Web

There is a reason why the verb for getting to know others who may be in a position to help you is called networking. When doing this activity, you are, in fact, working a *net* or a *web* of contacts. It's much like that old shampoo commercial--someone who can help you get hired might tell one friend, who tells one friend, who tells another friend, and so on.

Note that I don't call networking a funnel, nor a ladder. If you only network up your line of authority, you will be seen as a climber. People will think you only connect to others because of the power they hold. If you only network with those who work *for* you, people may think you lack the confidence to work or socialize with power players. And, if you only network vertically-- up the career ladder or down the career ladder--you will neglect valuable contacts with peers in other companies or industries.

In a web, you can work up, down, across, and even through the middle. In a web, if one string breaks, you can step across and find a different path. In a web, you are supported by the strength of multiple ties, none of which is your sole support.

You may be discouraged thinking about your own networking web. You might be thinking you don't know anyone other than the people at your current job. Perhaps you're an introvert and don't socialize much. All of that might be true. But when it comes to job searching, you are in a better position than you might think. Start where you are, and get moving!

You probably have more contacts in your networking web than you think. There are many more people you know besides those on your cell phone. Your goal is to identify who in your web can help you. Friends and family are a sure bet to refer you, so start with them first. Where do they work? Who do they know? Who do they go to church with? Start telling them now that you are looking. Be sure they hear in your voice that you are excited about a new opportunity. You don't need to tell them why you're looking if you were fired. Just tell them something vague such as, *It didn't work out.*

You also need to identify individuals who know you well enough to at least refer your name to a hiring manager or a recruiter. Well enough means a person who can provide at least one positive trait about you. Well enough might also be someone connected to a professional contact you know extremely well.

In my roles, I have frequently been asked for names of possible candidates. I am also asked by candidates to refer their names to other hiring managers. I am always happy to do both. Why? Because I know many people well enough to give their name to a hiring manager. All someone has to do is ask.

If I know the candidate well, I will provide my assessment as a reference. If I don't know the candidate well, I am still happy provide my impression of any limited interactions. For example, I might say, *I met Carla through my professional network. Although I've never worked with her and can't tell you about her professional skills, she always seemed very friendly and helpful.*

30

I'm not sure exactly what type of candidate you want, but her resume is worth taking a look at.

In order to get an idea who might be able to help refer you in this manner, I recommend that you actually draw a web of connections. Start with you in the center of the web. Now draw lines for friends and for friends of friends. Do the same with your family. Include their coworkers, bosses, and colleagues.

Be very broad in your thinking. It's not unrealistic for your aunt to ask a question on your behalf. (This is assuming your aunt loves you, and you got her a birthday card last year). She might say to her boss, *Hey my nephew Tom is looking for a new opportunity. He's a great guy with skills in sales and marketing. Do you know any other companies, or do you have any colleagues who are hiring in that area?*

If your friends and family are on good terms with their employers, their bosses could even call colleagues who are hiring. The boss could say, *I have the name of a guy who's looking for jobs in the area you're hiring. I don't know him at all, but his aunt is great. I'll tell her to have him send his resume to you.*

List the contacts your close friends and family have. Once you've identified those contacts, expand your web. Begin drawing lines that include your neighbors and people you exercise with. List fellow church/faith group attendees. Include members of professional groups you belong to and anyone else you come in contact with on a day-to-day basis. Write the companies these contacts work for. Try to remember anyone who mentioned a contact who might be hiring.

You won't ask these individuals for an actual reference. But you will ask them to let you know if they hear of a job opening. If there is a position available where they work, you could ask them for a referral. Say, *I know we haven't worked together, but*

I would like to ask you for a small favor. I would appreciate it if you could refer me to the hiring manager. I'm hoping if you do so, he might take a look at my application and resume. I know they get so many it's probably hard for them to screen through them all!

If you feel uncomfortable asking for a referral, think about how you would feel if you were asked. Usually, you are happy to help out someone--after all, you're only giving a name. It's just a small favor. People will feel the same when you ask them.

I know it feels difficult to ask for the favor of a referral. I know that when I was leaving my position, it felt weird to ask my colleagues for assistance. I forced myself to do so when an executive coach told me, in short, to "Get over it, Staci!" She emphasized that people are more than happy to help their colleagues when they can. She asked me to think of all the people I had helped or referred over the years. That did it for me. I asked.

The result was that one of my female colleagues referred me to a recruiter who was filling a position for a different organization. As I became a finalist for that position, a job opened up in her own company. I ended up selecting the job in the organization where she worked. This very busy colleague even went out of her way give me insights about the pros and cons of working for each organization. And all I had to do was ask.

In my example, did you notice that neither interview was offered based on my application? I received the interviews based on the referrals alone. Of course I had to complete an application and go through an interview process as well. But the referral was what got me through the door. Keep in mind, my colleague wasn't a close friend. She was just one person helping out another. You're going to find that along your job search. Once you put it out there that you're looking, you'll discover so many really nice people willing to help you. But did I mention... you *have* to ask!

When you finish drawing your networking web, you should have a list of 30 or more individuals who could at least refer your name. You should also have another 30 or so who might know of a job before it's posted, even if they don't know you at all. Begin calling or drafting emails to the first 30 people. Ask them if anyone in their own network is hiring. In addition, as you see jobs posted, think creatively about who you may know at that company--or who in your network may know someone.

Maybe you're applying to a pharmaceutical company and your brother-in-law is a nurse. It's worth asking if he knows anyone there. Perhaps you are applying for a city government job. If your best friend's dad works for the neighboring city, he might know someone through his professional network. If your neighbor's wife works in human resources for one hospitality company, she may know other human resources professionals at the competing hospitality company.

Your networking web will be the single greatest tool in helping your job search paperwork receive attention. Once you've been referred, be sure that your application, resume and cover letter all support others' positive opinion of you. Don't make the mistake of assuming you can slack on the paperwork just because someone provided your name.

Throughout the process, ensure that your professionalism and attention to detail are apparent. Any hiring manager who has received information about you will still scrutinize your paperwork. If it is anything less than excellent, you will let down the person who referred you.

How to Network at Work

Your work is the best place to expand your networking web, even if you are no longer employed there. Don't be afraid to ask former coworkers for help or referrals. If you were laid off and you know your supervisor was unhappy to see you leave, list that person as a reference. Ask him for referrals.

If you were not fired for misconduct, but your supervisor found your performance lacking, look elsewhere for a referral. It is entirely possible you can still find colleagues and higher-level employees who supported the work you were doing. They may be willing to refer you to other employers.

However you left your job, make a list of your allies at work. Include individuals who you know have contacts at other companies. For example, many people have spouses who work in competing companies, but in the same industry. They may have knowledge of upcoming vacancies in your line of work. Email them to ask if they would be willing to let you know if they hear anything. If they do hear of a potential job, request that their spouse put in a good word for you so that the hiring manager will review your resume.

Do the same with members of any professional organizations you belong to. Let them know that you have moved on from your previous organization and are looking for a new position. Let the group's leadership know that you are willing to give more time to help the organization while you're searching. Then ask them to let you know if they become aware of vacant positions. Ask if they would refer you.

If you are still employed and looking for a promotion, stay aware that networking happens every day. If you are nice to people, if you work hard, and if you help others, you have made a good start. If you create drama, get into arguments, and don't work as hard as others at your same level, that will get you known in the wrong way.

Always remember: the person you got snippy with yesterday may be the one telling a future boss *not* to hire you. Don't have bad days. If you can't have a great day, at least have a peaceful one. At the most basic level, networking at work is about ensuring that the people around you would be likely to refer you as a likable candidate and a good colleague.

When you know you want to promote or advance your career, embark upon very deliberate networking. Networking while employed is relative easy, because these are people who interact with you frequently.

Some people aren't sure how to approach powerful individuals who don't work at the same location. It's true that usually those in influential positions are very busy. Many times they are difficult to access because there are layers of people who work for them. Each layer has someone whose job it is to give the influential person more time for strategic endeavors. The more influential the person, the more layers you need to go through.

In these cases, unless you work for a very small organization, plan your networking strategy in advance. Prioritize influential individuals to contact as follows:

1. Within your departmental area, identify the company leader in charge of the department if that person interacts directly with your level of position by running meetings, setting strategy, or organizing departmental work. If you are at a level that does not interact with that person, choose the highest-level person in your department who guides your everyday work the most.

2. Also within your departmental area, identify influential people who are at your same level, who may be in a different business unit, and who you believe are likely to be promoted in the near future.

3. Going outside your departmental area, identify influential people who are no more than one supervisory level above your position.

4. Going outside your departmental area, identify influential people at your level who may have general insight into the company and who you believe are likely to be promoted in the near future.

Once you have identified these individuals, use multiple strategies to make the connection. These strategies will help them get to know you better. It can look odd if, out of the blue, you invite someone you don't even know for drinks. Thus, it is ideal if you have an authentic opportunity to meet the person such as in a meeting or at a professional event.

Offer to work on additional projects or serve on committees. Offer to help be a volunteer, note-taker, or logistical expert. Offer to investigate or research a specific idea or initiative in order to provide background or context. In short, make yourself available to do work that others don't have the time or the desire to do.

In this way, you will encounter influential leaders naturally. You don't have to force the initial encounter. When later you do request a one-on-one, ensure that there is a purpose for the meeting. Make sure it is a request the individual will find compelling and interesting.

In addition, I recommend only asking for a half-hour of their time. If the person is very busy, a half-hour won't seem too intrusive, but it will give you an opportunity to learn and make a connection. The following are potential reasons to ask for a meeting:

1. To gather the person's perspective on a specific initiative you are working on.

2. To gather the person's advice regarding potential career pathways within the company.

3. To gain the person's insight about your line of business or line of work.

4. To ask the person for advice regarding a decision you need to make, for example, deciding to take a promotion in one area or the other.

Finally, don't forget to network with those who hold positions that are at a lower level than yours. Some of the high fliers in that group could be in a position to refer you to your desired job at some point in the future. If you only interact with those in a higher or equal level position, you will be viewed as insincere. People may believe your sole purpose is to move up the career ladder.

Those in positions lower than yours might not be the ones actually doing the hiring. But they will certainly put in a good word for you if they viewed you as a trusted colleague or mentor. An added bonus is that it feels good to "pay it forward" to others and be the person they look to for a referral!

How to Network in the Community

Community organizations are a great place to network. It takes time outside of your workday, but volunteering has additional benefits. You feel good about helping the community.

You get to know others who are in situations far more difficult than your own. Many times you learn something new.

In addition, volunteering is something you can add to your resume if you have committed a lot of time or energy to one cause. Among the community organizations you might volunteer for, I recommend two primary organizations. The first organization is a church or any other spiritually based group, no matter what the denomination or type.

I recommend churches for several reasons. First, churches usually have a variety of volunteer options within them, so you can find something you like. Second, it's my observation that people who share your same spiritual beliefs are more likely to help you or refer you to a job. Third, members of churches usually represent a wide range of occupations, so you have more options available to you.

Finally, if you are attending a spiritual institution regularly, you will feel more comfortable asking for a referral. It's easier to ask someone you have interacted with over the course of a year rather than the people you might have just met when volunteering at another organization.

The second type of community organization I recommend is a large, nationally-recognized non-profit such as United Way, Goodwill or Habitat for Humanity. If you have smaller organizations you want to help, then of course do so. All volunteering will contribute positively to your job search efforts.

However, in order to maximize your networking opportunities, you are better off volunteering for a larger organization that contains multiple members. Remember, in addition to feeling good about yourself, you want to expand your networking web as much as possible. Your goal is to gain employment. Volunteering for these large organizations is one way to do that. When you do volunteer either for a spiritually-based organization or for a large non-profit, be sure to adhere to the following advice:

1. Be as dependable and reliable as you would on a job. You don't need to volunteer 40 hours a week there. But if you do commit to working all day on Saturday and Sunday, be sure to follow through.

2. Choose projects and time slots where you know others will be present. Obviously, the organization may need you to do some work that will be on your own. However, be proactive by sharing up-front that you prefer activities where you can meet and interact with others.

3. Get out of your comfort zone and introduce yourself to other people while you volunteer. Working alone or on a solo project is fine if your only goal is the satisfaction of volunteering. But if your goal is expansion of your networking web, it won't do you any good to work on your own.

4. Be nice and get along. Take great care to smile a lot, ask people about themselves, and offer additional help. Be flexible and be positive no matter what work you're assigned to do. Don't complain and don't be bossy.

5. Tell others you're looking for full-time work, but don't tell them too much. Your goal is for others to see you as a valuable asset who is on a break from full-time work. It doesn't help you to go into detail about why you were let go, how long you've been looking, or how many interviews you've had and not gotten the job. Instead, focus on the positive. You could say, *It was a big transition to move on from my company, but it was a blessing. I've been lucky to have more time to focus on myself and to volunteer for some causes I believe in. Now I think I'm ready to get back to work full-time, so let me know if you hear of anything.*

Before You Start Networking Online

There are plenty of ways to use online networks to maximize your job prospects. Before you even think about using these strategies, be sure your online presence is professionally appropriate. Remove all of your Facebook posts, Snapchat stories, Twitter posts, and Instagram photos that show you drinking, smoking, scantily clothed, or making fake gangsta signs into the camera.

Review your profile names as well. If your Twitter profile is, for example, @RowdyPartyGirl, change it. Do you really want your future employer to think that's the way you describe yourself? Make sure any posts you have written avoid all political commentary and remove anything posted that could be perceived as being negative about any one group, political party, country or other affiliation.

When looking for a job, the only acceptable topics for public posts are family, friends, pets, birthdays, graduations, and those quirky cat videos that get shared and re-shared. Go to each of your social media feeds and delete any posts not appropriate for a seven-year-old. Think to yourself: Would I feel perfectly OK if this post was attributed to me on the front page of the newspaper? As a Twitter post shared with thousands of people? When in doubt, delete it out.

After you've deleted all potentially damaging posts, move your account settings to completely private during the time of your job search. Don't accept new friends/followers you don't know. Don't tag (name) others in your photos and posts. Whoever you tag or share your posts with can share what you've written with someone else. Because that can occur, I recommend you refrain from posting anything during the time you're looking for a job. Even better, deactivate your account until you find a new job. These recommendations aren't full-proof, but they will help discourage potential employers from digging too deep into your social media presence.

Next, Google yourself to see what comes up on the search. Your future employer will be doing it, so you want to know what comes up. Click on each result to review the content. If there is negative information about you on the internet, get prepared to explain the situation if asked. Don't address it at all in your paperwork, because it's unlikely the future employer would do a web search on your name before they interview. The background check will happen at the end of the process. At that time, you will be able to explain yourself as best you can.

There are also firms that help you remove negative or untrue content about you on the internet. These firms work in two ways. They work with online companies to get negative information removed. But they also use technology to help the good content about you appear first in a web search. Their rates vary depending on how many hours it takes to help you, and it can get very costly.

For that reason, if your online presence is truly terrible, consider changing your name legally. Yes, I mean it. I know it sounds like a drastic step, and it is. But it can be a lot less expensive than being out of work for several months. In a full background check, your employer will still be able to identify you via your social security number. They will still find any convictions. You will still need to give the names of your former employers. However, legally changing your name will help you recreate a neutral internet web presence. One step short of legally changing your last name, you could informally adopt your middle name as your first name. That won't be as effective, but it will help.

Taking this step will lessen the negative information a hiring manager would otherwise easily discover online. Most employers do not ask for your former name until you get to the background check process. If they do a standard web search before that, only pages with your new name will appear. And, if their background check is less than extensive, your new web presence might help you through that process as well.

Finally, if you have a relatively common name, be sure to click on all web search results for that name, even if they don't apply to you. If one of the people who shares your name has a very negative internet result, read each page. Could someone possibly think it was you?

For example, I hired a candidate from another state. There was someone with the same name, in the same state, and close to the same age as the person I hired. The online person had committed a terrible crime. At first, my team thought it was the candidate we had hired. Unfortunately for the candidate, the hiring process was delayed while we proved to ourselves there were two different people.

We did our due diligence—but some employers may not. Be prepared to tell your future employer that the terrible person online is not you. The usual time to do this is right before the background check process begins.

However, if you think your online doppelganger may be why you are not receiving interviews, call it to the attention of your future employer during the paperwork process. Use a separate sheet of paper. Upload it with your resume and cover letter. State simply, *I am aware that there is a person online with the same name as me. This person committed a crime. I want you to know that the person is not me. I will be happy to provide additional identifying details during the background check process in order to verify I am in no way associated with that individual.*

How to Network Online

After you've cleaned up your social media presence, the next thing you should do when you start looking for jobs is to create or update your LinkedIn profile. People are not going to hire you directly from LinkedIn. However, depending on your situation, recruiters may contact you for open positions. In addition, you can use it find out more about the type of people who work at specific companies. It's also useful because people may look at your profile there in order to gather more information about you. If they get the information there, they won't feel a need to go to informal places like Facebook and Instagram.

Don't identify yourself as unemployed on LinkedIn. List some sort of work that you are currently doing. It's common for people who are looking for full-time jobs to be consulting, writing, or furthering their education. It's always better to give the perception you're working while looking for a permanent position.

Be sure to update your LinkedIn profile with a high-quality photo that looks professional. You can have someone take the photo with a good phone-camera using portrait mode. Wear a suit jacket and make sure the lighting is good. The very best way to get great lighting as an amateur is to go outside when the sun has just gone down. You'll only get a small window of time before it gets dark, but it will be well worth it in terms of quality. Get a variety of close-up shots and crop it to the LinkedIn photo frame appropriately. Nothing says amateur more than an oddly cropped photo where your head looks tiny or your mouth fills up half the frame. If you can afford a little more money, have your photo taken by a photography studio at a department store or mall. If you can afford to have a professional photographer come to your house and take photos, that is even better.

After you've updated your LinkedIn profile, it's time to begin networking. The first thing to do is contact anyone in LinkedIn who is a recruiter for your type of position. This means human resources professionals, contract recruiters, or anyone else who may be in a position to hire. However, I recommend you only initiate contact with individuals who have the job title or primary job function listed as recruiter in their LinkedIn profile. This will help you focus your efforts. Only if you know that specific company or manager is hiring should you contact others.

When you do contact the individual, make it short. State you are in the market for a new job opportunity and that you would appreciate them letting you know if one is available in their network. Attach your resume. Then that's it. Your aim here is to get information on available positions you might not otherwise know about.

The next thing you want to do is to share with your personal network that you are looking for a new position. This should only be done if you have an obvious reason why you are looking, such as a layoff or a geographic move. To start, only ask for information on open positions. Ask for a referral if a person who tells you about a position knows the hiring manager or company.

Never announce on your social networks that you have been let go or were fired. Never trash your former employer and never say anything bad about your coworkers. Never complain about a hiring process or how poorly you were treated at an interview. This will prevent you from getting another job. You want everyone in your online social network to see you as a positive, productive employee. This is so that when the time comes, you might get a referral you need.

Take the Shortcut

1. Networking helps you make contacts who can help your paperwork get noticed by hiring managers.

2. Every day at work is a networking day. Use it to meet others who may be in a position to help you.

3. Because you are networking every day at work, avoid creating enemies who might speak ill of you to potential hiring teams in the future.

4. Network with people who have a higher-level position than you do, the same level position you do, as well as those who have a lower level position. You never know who may be able to refer you for a job.

5. When networking with very high-level people, try to find natural events where you can connect. When requesting a meeting, have a specific purpose.

6. Network with others who attend your church or your spiritual community because those people are more likely to recommend you for a job. There are also a wide variety of professions represented.

7. Network with large non-profit organizations and at large events to maximize your ability to meet people.

8. Sanitize your online presence before beginning your job search. Hire someone to do so if you must.

9. Never speak ill of any employer online.

Chapter Three

The Real Role of Paperwork

Thorough, detailed, professional paperwork can make the difference in whether or not you get an interview. I know people wonder, *Why do I have to submit all that paperwork? And what happens once I've submitted it?"*

This chapter will give you insight regarding the way your paperwork moves within a company. This insight will help you avoid frustration wondering what is happening. It will also bring clarity regarding why you need to do each step requested.

Although the steps may vary slightly depending on the size of the organization, most employers are quite similar. I will first tell you about the basic reason you have to submit paperwork. Then I will provide you with details regarding each stage of the paperwork process. I will describe what the employer is doing with your paperwork, from the time you hit submit to the time you interview.

For each step, I will explain who is likely to see your materials. I will explain the main purpose of that step and mistakes to avoid. Finally, I will explain common reasons why your application materials could be rejected at that point. After reading this chapter, you won't make those mistakes, and your application will move forward in the process.

The Purpose of Paperwork

Application paperwork has gotten more and more complicated over the past twenty years. Intuitively, you would think that technology would have streamlined the process. That didn't happen. The overarching reason for the increase in complexity is the advent of online applications.

Online applications made the process so easy that mid to large-size companies now receive far more applications than in the past. Because they could do so without impacting applicant numbers, for many positions companies increased the complexity of their applications. Now, the process itself is a screening tool. If you can't get through the application, you're out.

This is going to be a huge advantage to you! Why? Because, while a good portion of the other applicants are going to be confused, skip a section, or fill out the application wrong, you are not going to make their mistakes! And when you don't make their mistakes, you've automatically gotten to the next step in the process.

Did you pay attention to that last part? Yes, you read it correctly. Just by completing all portions of the application and proofing it, you'll be a big step ahead. When you become frustrated, realize that the more complex the application, the fewer the applicants. And the fewer the applicants, the better for your job search!

Hopefully by now, you've guessed that my most important piece of advice to you is to always complete each portion of the application, including any explanations requested. Leaving information blank means you haven't met the requirement for completion. Your application will be rejected, just like the people who unfortunately haven't read this book. Now that you realize why you have to complete each section, I'm going to describe the application processing steps in detail. This will help you understand why completion is so important.

Step One: Intake

After your application is submitted, step one is intake. When you submit an online application, you typically also submit your resume and a cover letter. Once you hit the send button, your materials go to a person who downloads your information in some fashion. Companies have a variety of on-line application software systems. Those programs add your name to a database.

Once the posting closes, or until an appropriate number of applicants have applied, there is a person who checks each application. The person ensures that your application is complete, that all answers and explanations have been provided, and that your cover letter and resume (if requested) have been attached. Newer application software usually won't let you submit the application if all the requirements aren't met. However, the person doing intake will review your answers to ensure that they appropriately address the question and make sense.

This is usually the step where something goes wrong. Paperwork gets missed and applications are dropped or lost. Organizations who get thousands of applications are particularly prone to this, no matter how smoothly the process usually runs. Plenty of people complain to human resources because they state they never knew their application was incomplete. They add that nobody in the human resources department informed them that something was amiss.

It is a huge mistake to assume that the intake person is responsible for telling you that your application is not complete.

You, and only *you,* are responsible for shepherding your application through the process. Most companies do not have enough staff to let candidates know if there is a problem with their application. Software systems can only do so much to flag portions that are incomplete. And, if you've misunderstood the question or typed one paragraph that belonged in the answer to another question, software isn't going to catch that. But you still may be disqualified because of it.

Be proactive during this step in the process. If you are unsure whether or not your application was received, email the address provided and ask. If you do not receive an auto-generated confirmation email or message once you've submitted your application, never assume it was received. Email or call the employer and ask the question.

Take the time to review the application before you submit it. Software systems almost always allow you to do this. Unfortunately, it's a step that many candidates ignore in their haste to get it done. Upload your application, cover letter, and resume together to ensure that all are considered at the same time. If you upload portions separately, some may be missed.

Unless specifically directed to do so, never mail your cover letter or resume separate from your electronic application. This makes it much more likely that your paperwork will be lost or delayed. You absolutely must learn how to create a .pdf version of your resume and your cover letter and upload them. Using a scanner to create a .pdf from your Word documents looks messy and unprofessional.

Again, ensuring your application materials have been received is your responsibility. Technology is imperfect. So are the busy individuals tasked with gathering applicant paperwork in large organizations. When in doubt, email or call to ensure your materials have been received and that there is nothing missing.

Step Two: Initial Review

Step two is the initial review. In some organizations, the same person who downloaded your application does this process. In others, once your application has been judged complete, it moves to another individual. Then it goes through an initial review.

The purpose of the initial review process is to ensure that candidates with completed applications meet the minimum qualifications for the position. At this stage, there is no determination regarding the relative quality of each candidate. This step is a more technical process whereby an individual looks at the minimum qualifications listed on the posting. Then the person compares the listed qualifications to those of the candidate who applied.

Many software systems have automated functions that complete this task initially. The review is done behind the scenes. For example, if you state you have five years of experience, and the position requires seven, you could automatically be rejected from further consideration.

When used, "minimum qualification" questions/surveys are usually listed all in one section and ask you to indicate a yes or a no. For example, they may ask, *Do you have a minimum of three years progressively responsible sales management experience?* If you do not, you will state no, disqualifying you from further consideration at that point.

When the process is not automated, an individual provides the initial review for minimum qualifications. A person looks at your experience and education and determines if you have met the criteria. When an individual provides the screening, there is some room for interpretation. Therefore, you must be clear about your qualifications. Read the job posting and make sure it is easy for the reviewing person to see that you have, for example, a Bachelor's degree if one is required.

Determining if a candidate's specific job title represents experience in a management or leadership role can be difficult for the reviewer. Thus, be clear about your job responsibilities. Include a description such as *This was a management-level position where I advised and worked closely with other leaders and employees.* In this way, there will be no confusion for the reviewer. You don't want the reviewer to be forced to interpret, for example, what a *Property Construction Lead* really is.

Errors in this step usually come from a lack of clarity--either on your part or on the reviewer's part. If you are the one indicating how much experience you have, be sure what you list matches the number of years required. If you know that some job titles are vague, explain them so it's clear that you meet the minimum qualifications.

If your job titles or positions require some sort of unique explanation best explained over the phone, then call the company. Ask to speak to the person who will be reviewing applications for that position. Then explain your situation.

Paid internships done while still in college are notoriously confounding to employers trying to figure out how much actual experience you have. Reviewers try to determine if the internship was more like a college class or more like actual experience. If you have that type of experience, be sure to call and explain it was a job for which you were paid.

It is fine to apply for a select number of positions where you do not meet the minimum qualifications, as long as you are reasonably close to meeting them. Just be aware that you will probably not be interviewed in the first round if there are many other candidates who met the criteria. Also, it's not wise to apply for a large number of positions where you don't meet the minimum qualifications. When you do, you run the risk of looking desperate and lacking judgment.

Step Three: Quality Review

Step three is the quality review. The purpose of the quality review step is to determine, among the qualified applicants, whose specific, unique experiences make them the *most likely* to be a *match* for the position. Once you have met the minimum qualifications, there is no automatic interview. It doesn't matter if you are the applicant who numerically exceeds the criteria by the highest amount.

For example, let's say the position requires a Bachelor's degree and you have a Doctorate. You are not getting extra points toward your chances of getting an interview. Similarly, if you have twenty years of experience and the position requires five, you are not automatically going to be the top choice for an interview.

The reason for this is that once minimums are met, screeners are looking for candidates who might meet unique needs for that specific position. Those needs are not the same as minimum qualifications. They are more like preferences. Sometimes the preferences will be noted on the job description, and sometimes not.

For example, imagine a private company attempting to get a government contract. The contract would require adherence to a new set of regulatory requirements. Perhaps among all the accountants currently employed, the company has no one who has worked in a highly regulated environment. The company doesn't know whether or not they will get the contract, so they don't list that as a preference on the job posting. The job description may say that all who apply must be Certified Public

Accountants. But the company has a unique interest in someone who has regulatory experience.

In that situation, someone who has twenty years of accounting experience may not be interviewed. But the person who has five years of accounting experience working on a government contract will be.

Candidates tend to confuse this step with the minimum qualification review. I have received many phone calls from applicants who complain, *But I exceeded the minimum qualifications! I have twenty years of experience! How could you not select me for a interview?* I then explain what the hiring manager may have been looking for, beyond the minimum qualifications. Then the candidate complains, *Well they didn't put that on the job description!*

These complaints show a lack of understanding about the process. Hiring managers will use preferences to screen *only* if they are able to get candidates who have the specific characteristic they desire. Hiring managers don't necessarily want to list their preferences. This is because they could inadvertently discourage candidates from applying. They don't want to have a small pool from which to select.

In general, employers can choose to *not* hire any individual, for any reason, so long as it's not a discriminatory reason or discriminatory hiring practice. Many candidates don't understand this. When a candidate demonstrates anger or makes sarcastic, inappropriate comments to the person reviewing their file, that in itself can be a reason not to hire. I am shocked by the number of candidates who think they can demonstrate such behavior and still be hired.

The process of determining who has the greatest potential to do the job varies slightly across organizations. Sometimes the human resources team does it. Sometimes the actual department hiring does it. In larger organizations, a person in corporate human resources may conduct an initial quality review and recommend a group of candidates to the hiring manager. Then the hiring manager does another review to select individuals for the interview.

To increase your chances of receiving an interview, try to contact the actual person doing the hiring for that position. You may need to ask human resources who that is, if it's not obvious from the job posting. For example, perhaps the employer is a large hotel chain. The person doing the hiring, however, is the general manager of a specific hotel. In that case, first try to find out who the general manager is. Try to obtain his/her email address from the hotel website. If that doesn't work, try calling. Your email or phone call should be short and to the point. The idea is to put your name into the person's head so he/she might be more likely to interview you.

There are few errors in the process itself once an application has made it this far. If you don't get an interview, it may be because you haven't appropriately described your qualifications. Take the time to ensure that the experiences listed in your application paperwork match what is needed.

Accept that you could also be excluded from the interview process for no other reason other than you lacked qualities or experiences preferred by the organization. For example, when I left the field of government/education human resources, I'm sure some employers worried that I had no private industry experience. So they didn't interview me.

From an employer's standpoint, it makes sense. Among the people who meet the minimum qualifications, employers prefer individuals who have experience in that specific industry. If they can find such candidates, they are going to give them preference for an interview.

There are so many factors you can't predict at this step in the process. It would be difficult to list them all. I strongly believe that you will only create stress for yourself if you lament or try to control situations that, ultimately, have very little to do with your qualifications. If you know you have done everything possible to help your application stand out, let go of any disappointment you may feel. Move on to the next opportunity.

Take the Shortcut

1. The complexity of application paperwork has increased with the widespread use of online software.

2. Completing long application processes is sometimes part of the screening itself. This can work to your advantage, because other candidates won't do it.

3. In the intake process, ensure your application materials are complete. Submit all materials together. Follow up with a phone call if you are unsure whether or not your application was received.

5. During the initial review process, someone will match your qualifications to the minimums required on the job posting. Make it clear to the reviewer that the experiences you have meet the minimum qualifications for the position.

6. During the quality review process, the screener will determine who has the best potential to be a match for the unique needs of the position. After you've done your best to accurately represent your experience, stay positive if you don't get an interview. There could be other needs for the position that are out of your control.

Chapter Four

All About Applications

Your application will be reviewed during the intake process. It could also be reviewed later, by the hiring manager. As part of these reviews, your application will also be scanned to for any red flags such as unexplained gaps in employment. For this reason, you must ensure that your application is clear, accurate, and complete.

In this chapter I give you tips for preparing your application efficiently. Then I will provide you with directions for completing the common sections of any application you encounter. Finally, I provide additional miscellaneous suggestions to ensure your success.

Efficiency Tips

You will be asked to provide multiple pieces of information throughout the application process, including work experience, supervisors, and degrees. You will need to have dates, addresses and phone numbers for each.

Have all this information handy and in one place before you begin. Otherwise, you'll waste time looking up each of them every time you apply. Keep the information in an easy to access file so that you don't have to look for it with each new application. Also keep explanatory disclosure paragraphs, essay questions, and any other important information you might need to use for multiple employers.

Some online applications ask you to upload your resume so that the application software will pre-populate the information for you. Others will import your information from LinkedIn. Do not ever assume that your work is done at that point. While these functions can be helpful, they do not replace the detailed work you need to do.

You have to ensure the accuracy of the uploaded information. Invariably, you will need to clean up any errors that occurred in the translation. You may find that fixing the errors in the imported information takes more time than simply typing it in yourself.

Some people think that the best way to fill out paragraph-type questions is to write them in a word processing program like Microsoft Word and spellcheck them. Then they cut and paste the paragraphs into the application. That is better than not spellchecking at all.

However, the best way is to type the paragraph *first* into the on-line application. Then cut and paste it to a Word document to check your spelling and grammar. If your writing tends to contain a lot of errors not caught by automated checking, be sure to have someone else edit it as well.

The reason why you type it into the online application first is to avoid any formatting errors. When you type it first into Word, hidden formatting can make your paragraph and sentences look odd when you move them back into the application. If you really want to use Word first, make sure you choose the *undo formatting* option. That way, what you cut and paste is less likely to appear strangely in the online document.

Work History

I have never seen an application that asks you to list your experience in chronological order, from the first job you've had forward. Ever. Assume that all applications expect you to start with the most recent job first. Work your way backward from there. That said, do read the directions to be sure the application fits the normal format.

If you are newly out of college, then your work history will probably not be extensive. If you are filling out an application for your career job, you can avoid listing small summertime jobs. Use them, however, if they pertain to the job you want.

For example, let's say you have a microbiology degree, but you've decided to go into human resources in the hospitality/gaming industry. In that case, you would probably focus on the jobs you held during college which were service industry oriented. You might also focus on jobs or projects where you conducted training or selected candidates for a grant or a program.

Some people have jobs where they work for one general employer but are assigned to different business units. For example, if you work for an agency that places temporary workers, you work for that agency. But you may have served extended time periods at specific businesses. For this and similar situations, list the company who issues you the paycheck as the employer. Then, list your longer-term assignments in the *job responsibilities* area.

First write your general tasks, such as, *I provided clerical assistance to various employers such as....* Then list each business and how long you were there. This shows the screener that you were well liked enough to have been offered longer assignments at companies.

58

In the work history section, applications ask you who your current supervisor is. Then they usually ask, *May we contact this supervisor (or employer)?* This poses a dilemma if you know your current supervisor will not say positive things about you.

With a few exceptions, marking *no* on this question will be a red flag for those screening your file. Providing an explanation is problematic if your reason is that *My supervisor and I do not get along,* or some version thereof. I highly recommend that you mark yes on this question even if you know your supervisor will not be positive.

The reason for this advice is that future employers will most likely not contact your current employer during the screening process. If they do contact that employer, it won't occur until after you have been selected for the new position. If you mark *no* at this step, it will make them wonder if there is a problem at your current position. Marking *yes* allows you to move forward in the process.

Once they have interviewed you, selected you, and are beginning the reference/background check process, then you should tell the hiring manager about your relationship with your current supervisor. You might say, *One of the reasons I was looking for a new position was because of my relationship with my supervisor. I can give you the names of other colleagues who would provide a more positive reference.* Hopefully at that point the future employer is invested enough in you that they will contact other references.

In addition, many companies no longer complete formal, traditional reference checks. Reference checks create delays in the hiring process, are notoriously inaccurate, and they add greatly to human resources labor costs. So your future employer may not even do a reference check. However, if they see that you mark *no* to the *May we contact this supervisor/employer?* question, they may try to get additional information.

This question also poses a problem for individuals who do not want their current employer to know they are looking. If you mark no on this question, be sure to explain why, if the application gives you the space to do so. If you do not want your employer contacted during the early stages, but he/she could be contacted if you are a finalist, mark yes. Then write, *This supervisor may be contacted if I am a finalist for the position.*

Most managers understand that applicants want to prepare their supervisor for a phone call in the event the applicant is selected as a finalist. If you work for a company that terminates any individual who is actively pursuing other employment, take a more active role in explaining the reason why you marked no. If the application does not give you space to explain fully, include it at the beginning of the *position responsibilities* section. Then follow up with a phone call to ensure someone doesn't inadvertently miss that you marked no.

Experienced human resources personnel are familiar with these situations and are used to working around them. Marking no on this question because you'll be terminated if your employer knows you're looking is a valid reason. It should not hinder your ability to get an interview.

Work history sections also usually ask you to explain why you left each employer. Obviously, if you are still employed, you will write, *Still employed by this company.* For each of the employers you left, frame the reason for your departure so that it will seem positive, or at least neutral.

If you moved for a promotion or because you moved cities, indicate those as reasons. Never write, *I was fired* unless specifically asked if you were terminated. Further, never write, *I quit because it was an intolerable situation.* Both of those reasons are likely to prevent you from getting an interview.

Instead, make a more general statement. Use phrasing that is open to interpretation. Examples are, *I left this position and pursued a different career path* or *After new management took over, I left the company.* Both sentences are truthful without giving information that is unhelpful to your job search.

At some point you may need to explain in greater detail why you separated from that employer. Usually the application process you won't require you to do so. Still, you'll want to be prepared for the question to be asked at any time in the process. Before answering, re-read Chapter One to refresh your memory regarding how to frame a negative departure from any employer.

Finally, work history sections usually ask you to explain any gaps in employment. You do not need to explain the reason for the gap if it would be would be viewed as negative. For example, you wouldn't say, *I was let go from my position and was looking for work.* Instead, explain what you were doing during the gap. You might say, *I was attending additional professional development which would help my career path.* Perhaps during the time you were looking for work, you were helping to care for a sick relative. You could say, *My help was needed to take care of my grandmother in the last stages of life.* The point is to have a truthful yet neutral reason for not working during the gap.

Many people have lengthy gaps in employment, such as would be the case for parenting. If that is your situation, take the opportunity to reiterate and explain other work you did during the time period. It is helpful if you volunteered at your child's school, did clerical work for a volunteer organization, or served on a non-profit board.

That work helps show that you have recent skills. It also shows that you went above and beyond, even during your busy parenting time away from work. If the gap was lengthy due to a geographic move, be similarly descriptive about your work-related activities during that time period.

Education History

Education history sections are fairly straightforward. You will typically be required to verify you have a high school diploma or equivalent. Then you will be asked to list any additional education you have obtained. In the education section, it is important to ensure your education level matches what is required on the job posting. Once you've done that, list your education in chronological order unless the directions say otherwise.

One of the more confusing aspects to listing your education is what to do if you have taken several courses from multiple colleges/universities, without working toward a degree. Sometimes you've taken an on-line course or a weeklong course for which you received college credit or CEUs (Continuing Education Units). Use your discretion about how to list them. If you've only taken a few, it makes sense to list each one of them. If you've received multiple college credits in that fashion, try to list them as one unit, with each course bulleted out.

The problem is that most education sections require you to choose dates, universities, and major/minor areas from a drop-down menu. Usually the software won't allow you to use free form text. Adapt what you can. Any non-degree coursework you cannot list in this section, add to your resume.

People also get perplexed about how to list a major or minor area for colleges if there was not a specific area of focus. If the section does not allow you to leave it blank, choose anything that somewhat matches your coursework. During the background check process, most companies are only going to check that you attended and, if applicable, that you earned a degree. Unless it's required for the job, employers are not going to count up your coursework in each area to determine themselves exactly what your area of focus was.

If you aren't sure of the exact day or month for any given course, you can list an approximation. It's best if you know exactly, but you won't be disqualified from a job if you are off by a month or two. Just be sure that you aren't inflating your time in college if you didn't earn a degree. If you do that, you could be disqualified for lying on the application.

Treat your GPA similarly, if the application asks for it. It's fine if you're off by a tiny bit, for example a 3.45 instead of you listing a 3.5. But if your GPA was 2.5 and you state it was 3.0, you will probably be disqualified or at least challenged for not being truthful.

Finally, be cautious listing your degree if you earned it from a fringe university that could be dubbed a diploma mill. These universities exchange time worked for a fancy paper diploma that means nothing. They use a mocked up transcript that reflects a minimum amount of actual college coursework (if any).

Organizations will not view you favorably if you try to pass off your diploma mill degree as a standard earned degree. If one of these "colleges" allows you to do an entire Bachelor of Arts degree in a year with only a few courses, you are better off saving your money. Employers who require a college degree know to look for diploma mill degrees. Spend your hard-earned dollars on actual coursework from a real college instead.

Even if the degree isn't required for your position, you could be disqualified just for listing it. In one instance, the finalist for a position had enough work experience so that a degree was not required. However, he listed the diploma mill degree anyway. The organization eventually pulled the job offer because they viewed it as a lie on the application.

Double-check the education requirements on the job posting. Most organizations require your degree to be from an accredited college or university. Standard accrediting agencies exist, and they cannot accredit diploma mill colleges and universities. As a result, these diploma mills make up bogus "accrediting" organizations that look official. If you don't know if your college might be considered a diploma mill, Google the name of the college and the word "diploma mill". There are a variety of websites that list them.

Criminal Disclosures and Drug Tests

Many positions require you to disclose if you have ever been arrested or convicted of a crime. The majority of employers only ask you to disclose arrests that resulted in a felony conviction. However, there are many exceptions.

Positions in highly regulated environments almost always require you to disclose any arrests or convictions other than misdemeanor traffic violations. These include positions in police, fire, and education. These also include employers who have sensitive government contracts for which you may need a specific level of security clearance. Finally, some industries require that those hired for certain positions be licensed, cleared, or certified via a state background check.

Each state varies, but commonly required licenses include all varieties of medical, dental, and psychological licenses, massage therapists, accountants, nail technicians, certain casino employees, and sometimes even dog groomers. If you are reading this before you've been arrested or convicted of any crime, then you are lucky. Having to explain on an application why you were convicted of indecent exposure because you couldn't find a bathroom at Mardi Gras does not make a good first impression on your employer. Similarly, arrests for misdemeanors relatively common in the teenage years still stand out on an application.

You must always disclose whatever the employer asks you to. Some might require only convictions. Others might require arrests and convictions. After you are hired, many employers do an extensive background check. It will reveal anything you neglected to on the application.

Once you have disclosed the arrest or conviction, be sure to explain it fully. If the crime occurred when you were an alcoholic, and you have been sober for ten years, that is a reasonable explanation. Depending on the employer, it may prevent you from getting an interview. Still, it is better than them finding out later during the background check.

Be sure in your explanatory letter that you go into detail regarding the steps you took to prevent the issue from happening again. Indicate your remorse as well. Take responsibility for what happened and focus on the changes you made in your life. Hopefully it was only a one-time occurrence. In that case, you will be able to show that you learned your lesson the first time.

I need to provide additional information regarding employers who conduct fingerprint processes. Fingerprint processes are reserved for certain special and highly regulated industries. But when an employer requires them, you need to know that *any* arrest that resulted in you being fingerprinted will most likely be provided to the employer. This includes any arrest that was later expunged from your record.

For example, let's say you were arrested for shoplifting and fingerprinted. Your attorney was able to get the conviction expunged from your record after a certain number of years based on good behavior. Your attorney will tell you that you don't have to disclose it, because it was expunged. That might be true for many employers, but not for those who fingerprint you. In the education industry, I frequently had to tell applicants, *The directions say you need to disclose any arrest. I didn't ask you just for convictions.*

For employers who fingerprint, you must always disclose everything. Even if you had a juvenile record sealed, there will be a notation on the report that one exists. The reason certain employers are able to ask for arrests and not just convictions is due to the nature of the position.

If you are applying for a position that works directly with money, your employer wants to know if you have had multiple arrests for theft, even if none of those resulted in a felony conviction. The same is true for positions working with children. One DUI pled down to reckless driving may not be of large concern, but more than one might.

Keep in mind that employers must be careful if they do exclude you from employment solely on the basis of an arrest or conviction. Applicants have won complaints filed with the Equal Employment Opportunity Commission (EEOC) when certain employers had no business need for a blanket denial of any applicant with a criminal record. The reason for this is that blanket denials tend to have an adverse impact on certain groups of individuals in protected classes. If you are applying for a large company, be reassured that only certain crimes will prevent you from employment.

Drug tests can also be used as part of the hiring process. Due to their expense, they are almost always used only after you are the selected candidate. The extent to which tests look for certain drugs varies. Driver positions, those operating heavy machinery, and public safety positions will do a full testing panel which includes common prescription medications such as Xanax and Ambien (and their generic forms).

Most drug tests are only looking for illegal drugs. If you use illegal drugs, don't waste your time applying for employers who drug test, unless you've been clean for several months. Despite what you read online, you are not going to be able to beat the test. And if you fail, you will have prevented yourself from any future employment at that company.

One applicant received a fairly high-level management position. He began to relocate his family, and he quit his previous job in preparation for the move. His drug test came back positive for an illegal drug. His offer was rescinded. Although he stated he was now clean, the drug test indicated otherwise. Had he waited several months before applying, he would not have burned a bridge with the hiring company.

Marijuana, formerly an automatic disqualifier, no longer is in some states. However, employers can still deny employment to someone who tests positive for marijuana. It can be problematic for the employer if the marijuana use is for medical purposes, but some still try. However, in states where it is legal, many employers have chosen not to disqualify applicants because of marijuana use, except for safety sensitive positions where individuals drive frequently or operate dangerous equipment.

There are differences in the way employers view even legal marijuana use. Thus, I still strongly recommend that you discontinue using it while you are applying for positions. You usually don't know what the policy is when you apply to a company. And it's not a good idea to ask, unless you find someone who will give you the information privately. Assuming you aren't addicted, you should easily be able to give up recreational use until you obtain a job.

Other Application Tips

In this section I list several other miscellaneous tips with regard to the filling out applications. Keep these in mind as you complete any application, and you will be more likely to get an interview.

First, your application for any one company should be updated each year if you apply several times and don't get a position. Many companies will purge your application if you don't log in for a certain time period. That's one reason to keep it updated. You don't want to redo the application all over again.

Another reason to keep it updated is that you always want your application to look fresh. You want your signature date to be current. Additional experiences and education should be added as well. More importantly, you don't want the hiring manager to think that you've been applying for a year with no results.

Next, there may be additional information, surveys or forms to complete which are unique to that industry. For example, some companies receive special tax breaks or advantages for hiring individuals who have recently been in a designated government program. These forms are always optional, but do fill them out. You never know if it might help get your name referred.

Another consideration is how to handle personality or skill-based inventories or surveys. Some measure basic skills such as English speaking ability or mathematical ability if required for the position. Others attempt to determine if your personality or mindset would be a good match for the position.

When these are part of an online application, you are usually redirected to another website where you take the test. If you look at the web address and on the webpage itself, you can determine the third-party company administering the assessment. Once you find that out, open another tab on your browser and search the web to find out more information about that specific test.

If it's measuring basic skills and you need to update your basic skills, first save your application for later. Then find a free online program that will allow you to practice your skills. Do not take the test if your reading, writing and mathematical skills are not up to par. If you do, you will fail the test and automatically be disqualified. You are better off waiting a day or two to submit the application after you refresh your skills.

If it's a personality test, find out the personality traits the test is measuring, if you can. The directions will tell you not to prepare for the assessment. They will direct you to simply choose the answer that most applies to you. As a whole that's good advice, and you should follow those directions. If you try to give them answers you think are what they want, your test can have inconsistent results.

Nevertheless, it can help you to at least know what they are measuring. If you can't figure it out from the test information on the web, read the job posting again. Then tailor your answers so that they match what the company is looking for, as stated on the job posting. Be cautious, however, that you're not changing your answers in a way that goes against your fundamental personality. Otherwise you could end up unsuccessful in a job that requires a mindset that you don't have.

Finally, for all but the smallest employers, there will be an optional Equal Employment Opportunity form. This form asks you to provide information about your race/ethnicity, your gender, your veteran status, if you have a disability, and if you are over forty years old. These are considered protected classes. This means these are people, as determined by the government, who have historically experienced forms of discrimination in the hiring process (and other processes).

If you are a Caucasian male, not a veteran, not disabled, and under the age of forty, you can decide whether or not you wish to disclose the information. If you are in any of the protected classes, you should always fill out this form and disclose your status. The reason you should do so is that the vast majority of companies do want to diversify their workforce, especially with regard to race/ethnicity.

Employers cannot waive minimum qualifications in order to hire diverse candidates. Nor can they set quotas or specific numbers of diverse candidates they have to hire. However, they can, in their recruiting, focus on diverse applicants and refer them to hiring managers for further consideration. The only way you can be referred as a diverse candidate is if the human resources department knows you are in a protected class because you filled out the EEO form.

Obviously, the concept of diversity is somewhat dependent on the geographic location of the employer. The concept also varies depending upon the current makeup of the company's workforce and the type of position. For example, there are so many female elementary school teachers that hiring more women is not diversifying the workforce. However, there are very few African-American or black individuals in that same job type. Thus, school districts will seek to diversify their workforce in that manner when they have a good candidate.

If you are a Veteran or you have a disability, many larger companies dedicate personnel specifically to assist you throughout the hiring process. Do avail yourself of those opportunities. Frequently the people who assist you have a direct line to human resources or to hiring managers. If you meet the qualifications for the position, they can refer you. This helps your name get recognized among what might be dozens of applicants.

Take the Shortcut

1. Have names, phone numbers, addresses and dates of employment and education history handy when you begin filling out applications.

2. Write any narrative information in the online application first, and then cut and paste it to a Word document for spelling and grammar checks.

3. Unless you'll be fired for looking for a job, always mark yes to *May we contact this employer/supervisor?* It will be a red flag if you mark no, and the employer will probably not call your current supervisor unless you are the final candidate.

4. Explain gaps in work history and separations from employers in a way that makes them appear as neutral as possible.

5. Make sure your education level matches what is on the job description, and ensure that any degree you list was not from a diploma mill.

6. Disclose all arrests and convictions if asked to do so. Explain them fully by focusing on your remorse and the

steps you've taken so that a similar crime will not occur again.

7. Avoid marijuana use while you are looking for a job, even if it is legal in your state.

8. Update your application each year to ensure it looks fresh to the hiring manager.

9. Research any special skill or personality tests before you take them as part of the application process.

10. Always disclose on the EEO form if you are a member of a protected class.

Chapter Five

The Roving Resume

Your resume is usually the one piece of paper all hiring managers review. The application tends to be lengthy and printouts are multiple pages long. But your resume should be relatively easy to read. As a result, hiring managers tend to look first at your resume.

Content

The template you use for your resume is not as important as the content you put in it. Two-page resumes are perfectly acceptable for experienced professionals, as long as the most important information is first. Three-page resumes are less desirable. But they are equally acceptable in some circumstances. If you have had multiple jobs, if you've published several books or articles, or if you've won multiple awards, you may need three pages.

Think of your resume the way a hiring manager would see it. What's the most important piece of information? Your work experience, if you have it. Yet numerous resume templates have you listing your education first. If you're a new college graduate with no experience, that might make sense. If you're experienced, always place your education after your work experience.

After your name, the first thing the hiring manager should notice on your resume is what you can do. The best way to do this is to make three columns at the top of your resume. Each column should contain a skill you can do. For example, a human resource professional might list skills including collective bargaining, compensation analysis, employee relations and talent acquisition.

This method highlights the wide variety of skills you have mastered. It also ensures that the reviewer can scan your resume and very quickly see if you have skills the company is looking for. If you have limited work skills, you can add positive personality attributes here as well. Examples include collaborator, team player, and strong work ethic.

If you have no experience whatsoever because this is your first job, you can list your skills under your education. Highlighting your competencies in this manner points to the specific skills you learned in college. This is far better than only stating you have a business major. Google is your friend if you're unsure what to write. Enter the type of job along with the words *skills needed,* and various websites will give you some ideas. Use the phrases that truthfully describe you. Avoid using phrases that stretch the truth.

Be sure not to over-inflate your experience in the words you use. For example, it would be fine to list negotiation skills. It would not be fine to list interest-based bargaining, if you haven't done it. The first implies that you have negotiation skills and those could apply to a number of areas. That is appropriate. The second implies that you have actually done interest-based bargaining, which inflates your level of experience.

Formatting

After your name and your skill list columns, you'll list your employment history. Under each employer, list your accomplishments and responsibilities. Don't only list your job title. What you are able to do is not contained in the word *Sales Manager*. Nor is it contained in the word *Business Major*. Therefore, you must clearly show the application reviewer what you actually did in each job.

In order for any hiring manager to know if your experiences and skills match what they need, you must be very specific in telling them. Job titles alone do not tell the company what you have accomplished. This is because responsibilities of job titles vary across companies.

Some people have experience that is somewhat limited. You still need to take the time to bullet out as many different responsibilities as you can under each job you've had. Don't just say what the role was--say what you *did* in the role. You want the hiring manager to understand that although you may not have had a lengthy career, your previous jobs covered many areas of responsibility.

Once you have your template resume created, you need to adapt it to each job you apply for. Rearrange the skills each time you apply for a different position. Prioritize the skills the new employer states they are seeking by listing them first. Do the same with the accomplishments and responsibilities you list in the work history section. List first the responsibilities that were prominent on the job posting. Remove bullets or accomplishments that are unlikely to impress that employer. Replace them with accomplishments more focused on the job posting.

If you're going to use a skill list at the top of your resume, that will always come first after your name and contact information. Then, list your related professional experience if you have it. Start with your most recent job and work your way back. After your work experiences, provide your education. After your education, if you have multiple items in any of the following categories, list them in this order: publications and presentations, awards and recognitions, volunteer and community involvement. At the end of your resume, write *References Available Upon Request* or list your references.

If you're a recent college graduate with limited related work experience, you may list your education first. Put your special skills and talents bulleted underneath, if you didn't put them in columns at the top. However, only do so if you have no related work experience at all. If you had an internship or even a small project related to your college major, use those as your first work experiences. Your main concern as a recent college graduate is showing the resume reviewer that you have work experiences and skills that go beyond your college major alone.

When creating your resume, use a template readily available in Word. You can also create something for yourself after doing a web search for ideas. Search for a template that looks good to you, and then replicate it. It should be easy to read with normal margins and a ten or twelve point font. Try a few different formats to see which one looks better with the information you need to present.

Finally, have someone review your resume. Tell the person to look for typos, grammatical errors, and overall readability. In the era of online applications, your resume doesn't need to stand out as much as it needs to be easy to read. It needs to reflect the skills and experiences the future employer wants in an applicant.

Tips

Here are some general tips to keep in mind when creating your resume:

1. Never include your photo with your resume, unless of course the position requires it.

2. When you list each page number, write your last name beside the page number. This is important in case your resume pages get printed out with a stack papers. The hiring manager can then easily put it back together.

3. When uploading a resume, always create a new resume by using the *Save as* function and titling the document with your last name and the name of the company. This helps the hiring manager keep track of your electronic file if downloading. It also helps you be sure you are using the correct resume for that company's job.

4. Avoid using catchy graphics which can distract from the content, unless for a position that this would be expected, such as a graphic designer position.

5. If you have space on the second page, or if you need to fill up space on the third page, list the names and contact information of your references there. If you don't have space, write *References Available Upon Request*. Read the job posting expectations, however, to provide what is required.

6. Always upload your resume as a .pdf or similar file so that your tabs, bullets, and indentations will be accurately maintained.

7. Bring copies of your resume to your interview and offer them if it's clear the panel does not have a copy handy. This will assist them in remembering your experiences and skills.

Take the Shortcut

1. Adapt your resume each time you apply for a new position in order to highlight your skills and experiences each specific employer wants.

2. Ensure your resume is easy to read, clear, and provides detailed information regarding the skills, experiences and accomplishments you have.

3. Avoid photos and other quirky resume gimmicks. Keep your resume as simple as possible unless otherwise expected by the type of position.

Chapter Six

The Cover Letter

The cover letter introduces you to the hiring manager. Human resources is unlikely to read the cover letter thoroughly during the intake phase. This is because, at that point, they are only looking to determine if you meet minimum qualifications. However, quality review screeners and hiring managers will almost always read the cover letter. It gives them insight into your personality and thought processes. This helps them determine if you are more or less likely to be a match.

Content

You will waste time on the cover letter if you don't use it as an opportunity to clearly outline why your previous experiences and your work mindset are the perfect match for the job posted. Before you write the cover letter, have the job posting in front of you. Make notes on the job posting where your experiences look almost exactly like the responsibilities listed. Use a separate coding system to identify the areas that you may not be a match for. Finally, code those responsibilities that are similar to your work experiences, even if they are not an exact match.

The next step is to review the company's mission statement, values, vision, or goals. You can usually find versions of these on the company's website by looking in the employment or careers section. If a mission or values statement is not listed explicitly, look for broad statements about the company. This might include the company's purpose or what they strive to provide their customers. If all else fails, type in the company name in your search engine to determine if the company has been in the news or other publication. This should give you some insight about the culture or the company's critical business concerns.

Once you've gathered information, jot down ideas regarding why the company mission statement, goals or values are important to you. Write any life or work experiences that would support your commitment to the same values.

Formatting

A standard cover letter would be organized in this manner:

1. Opening paragraph: Tell why you want to work for the company in this role. Emphasize your commitment to their vision, mission, goals and/or values. End the paragraph with what you could contribute.

2. Second paragraph: Explain how your experiences are directly tied to the job responsibilities. Also include those that are similar. If you are new to the job market, this paragraph could show what your work strengths are. Use experience examples from your college activities, a work internship, a training program, or a team sport.

3. Third paragraph: Explain how your work habits, personality, and mindset match will help you transition smoothly to a new role in that company. Include how your personality strengths will help you begin contributing value right away.

4. Fourth paragraph: Explain any unique situations like your gap in employment, your imminent move to the company's

geographic location, or why you are willing to take a pay cut. You don't need this paragraph if you have nothing to explain.

5. Ending paragraph: Summarize your commitment and ask for the opportunity to interview.

Once you have mastered the organizational strategy to write a cover letter, you will find that it's quite easy to adapt your letter to each job posting. Although you will need to change the specifics to ensure that you're speaking to that position's requirements, your overall purpose for each cover letter is the same.

For most jobs, this format will successfully show the hiring manager how your experiences match the position, which is the main goal. There is no need to add large doses of cleverness and creativity. You don't know how your humor or creativity will come across, and you don't want to risk being screened out because a hiring manager determined you sounded weird.

That said, for some positions and companies, you'll want to add a dose of cleverness, usually in the opening and closing. How do you know when a level of creativity will be expected? Usually, you'll know if any of the indications are present.

First, if the job posting itself is clever and humorous, that is an indication of the company's culture. You should add humor to your letter in a way that matches the tone of the job posting. Second, use creativity if the type of job itself requires creativity. This could be true for a writing position or a position in the creative, graphic, or performing arts. Add the same level of creativity that is evident in the job expectation. Finally, your research may have indicated that the company has a reputation for quirkiness, humor, or a unique work environment. In that case, adapt your letter accordingly.

Ten Cover Letter Tips

Here are ten important considerations to keep in mind when writing a cover letter.

1. Double and triple-check your letter to be sure that the company name is correct throughout the letter. When you are adapting previous letters, it's easy to miss a change, and that will prevent you from getting the job.

2. When uploading a cover letter, use an electronic signature and save the document as a .pdf rather than scanning an original. This will make the letter look better when the hiring manager reads it. Also make sure you properly title the file with your last name and the words *Cover Letter.*

3. If there is no address on the job posting, use memorandum format rather than letter format. In the subject line, write the name of the job for which you're applying. Include a job posting number if there was one on the job announcement. This will ensure that your letter won't get misplaced if the company prints it out.

4. Also double and triple check spelling, grammar and punctuation. No matter how well you edit yourself, it's always best to have someone review it for you with a fresh set of eyes.

5. Focus only on why you match the expectations on the job posting. Only use personal information if it's required to explain gaps in employment such as taking care of a sick parent, raising children, or making a geographic move.

6. Resist the urge to explain why you parted ways with your previous company, even if you feel you were wronged. Focus on the positive and explain only what you need to if and when you are asked in an interview.

7. Always read the entire job posting to see if there are any specific directions or additional information you need to provide as part of the application process. If the information is best provided in a cover letter, be sure to include it.

8. It is ideal to keep your cover letter to one page. If you simply cannot do that, never write more than 1.5 pages. If it gets any longer, no one will read it.

9. Use clear writing. Avoid long sentences as much as possible. Overly wordy and complicated sentence structure is distracting to hiring managers. They want to quickly review materials rather than reading them thoroughly.

10. Use a clear, common font such as Times New Roman, Arial or Calibri. Never use scripted, italic, all bolded fonts, or all capital letters.

Take the Shortcut

1. Use the cover letter to explain clearly how your experience directly relates to the job requirements.

2. Unless expected by the company or industry, avoid gimmicky or clever themes or comments not related to the position posting.

3. Avoid common mistakes and errors by carefully reviewing your letter in advance of sending it, and have others review it for you also.

Chapter Seven

Common Mistakes

In this chapter, I explain several common mistakes that are made by candidates as part of the application process. These are easy to avoid. Review the list and make sure that you aren't inadvertently preventing yourself from getting to the next step in the process. When you make these mistakes, receptionists, human resources intake specialists, screeners and hiring managers are much less likely to recommend you for further consideration.

Don't Make These Mistakes

1. *Not reading directions that clearly tell you what to do, if only you had read them.* It's not terrible to call human resources if a part of the application confuses you. Before you do so, read the directions again, and look for any pop-up boxes that will explain it further. If you are constantly calling human resources because you don't understand how to use a pull-down menu, upload a resume, or enter a date in the right format, find a friend to help you instead. You don't want the employer to think you are technologically challenged.

2. *Not filling out the entire application.* There is a reason companies ask for the information. Most online applications now won't let you submit until all of the information is complete. If you don't have anything to say in a required section, write *N/A* or *Not Applicable*.

3. *Not providing enough information when the application asks for it.* This pertains mostly to explanations regarding gaps in employment, terminations, and criminal convictions. Be sure you have clearly explained the situation, and use complete sentences.

4. *Making typos or other errors on the application.* If you can, print out a draft of the application to preview it that way.

5. *Being unclear in how you list your experience.* Always list the most recent position first, unless otherwise indicated. Also be sure to clearly explain overlapping employment scenarios where you worked for multiple companies at once. If you don't explain the overlapping dates, it can be confusing for the screener.

6. *Relying on an old application that isn't updated.* If you apply for multiple positions at the same organization, be sure you update your resume and application each time to reflect current dates, job responsibilities and personal information. Otherwise, it will be obvious to the screener that you've been applying without success for a lengthy period of time.

7. *Not providing recommendation letter writers with the job posting and your resume.* Letters of recommendation are becoming less and less common, but some employers still require them. If the application process requires letters of recommendation, be sure that your writers have a copy of the job posting and your resume. Then ask them to focus their comments on the areas required in the job posting.

8. *Not updating letters of recommendation from year to year.* Ask your reference writers to simply change the date on the letter already written, so that it appears new.

9. *Planning vacations during the time period when you're actively looking for work, unless you know for sure there will be*

no interviews a certain week. Unless you're okay with missing out on an interview, you shouldn't plan vacations while you are looking for a job. If an employer calls you for an interview and you're on vacation, it's unlikely they will delay their timeline until you get back.

10. *Looking sloppy or strangely dressed when you come in to drop off items or ask questions of the employment center.* Any time you have an occasion to meet with your potential employer, you should be neatly dressed. You don't need to put on your interview suit, but at least put on a nice pair of pants and a clean shirt.

11. *Bringing disruptive and naughty children when you come in to ask questions.* If you're having trouble with the application and need assistance, make sure your children are old enough to wait quietly for you. Ideally, leave them at home. Application personnel are usually very busy, and they won't have time to pacify your children while you get help.

12. *Having your husband, wife, mother, father or other friends and family be an active participant in the application process.* If you get help from family and friends, the employer should not notice their assistance. If you have a question about the application or the process, you are the one who should call, not mom.

13. *Failing to explain something fully on the disclosure.* If you fail to explain a circumstance that requires an explanation, your application will be delayed or even disregarded.

14. *Using non-work-related individuals as work references.* This may be necessary if you are just entering the job market. However, be sure that the individuals you list are able to speak specifically to your potential in the workplace.

15. *Being rude to office staff when you need help with the application.* Every time you interact with the employer, consider it part of the selection process. Front office staff will tell their bosses if you are rude, and no one wants a rude coworker.

16. *Waiting until the last minute when the job closes and then needing help with the application.* Your crisis is not the fault of the employer. Avoid this possibility by applying for positions as soon as they open so that if you need help, you have plenty of time to get it. Also, some positions are only posted for one or two days even though they say, *Open until filled.* This is because the employer is getting so many applications that they can close the job in a few days and still have plenty of candidates. Don't miss out on the opportunity by delaying.

17. *Complaining that you didn't get an interview (rather than inquiring).* It's fine to inquire about the status of your application and to ask if there is anything that wasn't clear. Complaining that you didn't get an interview is inappropriate and will not help your case with that employer.

18. *Using weird phrases, nicknames, and stories within the application.* Some applications require you to answer questions in short-essay format. Be sure that the examples or stories you provide in these essays are engaging and interesting. But be sure they are appropriate. A good rule of thumb is if you're wondering whether or not to provide the story--don't. Use a different one.

19. *Using a strange email address that could be interpreted as sexual, offensive, or just plain weird.* For example, I encountered a personal email address that contained the phrase *LongFlute.* The person was a musician outside of his regular position. But if future employers saw that email address, they might find it offensive. Similarly, even if you were born in 1969, never use 69 in an email address. Other numbers/phrases which some may find offensive, no matter why

you personally use them: 420, XXX, and 911. Your friends may find you hilarious, but your future employer may screen you out because they think you lack good judgment.

For those in the younger crowd, you may have a funny X-Box gamer tag. Do not use it in the personal email address you use on a job application. The safest email address is your name at Gmail, Hotmail, Outlook or another current, popular online email provider. Using your birth year in the name will tell the employer your age, which usually should be avoided. Finally, using your AOL email account immediately tells your future employer that you are over the age of forty and don't use technology that much. (Are you really still accessing the internet through AOL?)

20. *Using text talk, emojis or abbreviations throughout the application.*__Occasionally you may need to abbreviate something in a portion of the online application itself. However, in general use formal writing structures and avoiding any abbreviations you might normally use in a text message.

Take the Shortcut

1. Avoid common errors to ensure that nothing in your application materials will prevent you from receiving an interview.

2. Remember that any time you meet with the employer, it is part of the selection process. Dress appropriately and demonstrate appropriate business behavior.

3. Keep all your paperwork updated to ensure your application appears current and that hiring managers won't interpret that you've been unsuccessfully looking for a job for a long time.

Chapter Eight

If You're Not Getting An Interview

When you've put in applications to several positions and haven't received even one interview, it's time to figure out why. In this chapter, I will give you strategies for following up and how to ask for feedback on your paperwork. Then I will provide you with some common reasons why you might not be getting an interview, so that you can alter your job search accordingly.

How to Follow Up

In order to find out why you haven't been getting interviews, you don't need to call every employer to get information. However, you may need to call several in order to get just one response.

Use a leveled approach to your questioning. Be careful to inquire without sounding upset and without accusing the company of being stupid for not giving you an interview. Start with a simple phone inquiry such as, *I'm following up to find out the status of X position, which I applied for.* Most employers will give you an answer to that question, telling you if the position has been filled or not.

Once you have them on the phone, you can try to follow up with a more detailed inquiry. You could say, *Would you mind looking at my resume and application and providing me with any suggestions regarding how I could represent my experience better?* Notice two things about this strategy. First, you'll inquire over the phone. Most employers are not going to give you any feedback in writing or via an email. Second, you start with a simple question. Then you use the opportunity to ask for advice. You don't make statements regarding your opinion of their selection process nor the fact that you weren't selected for an interview.

If you get this far with the employer, you'll probably get useful information. If your paperwork looks fine, usually they will tell you. If they tell you there were portions of your paperwork you could improve, you can edit those areas the next time you apply. In some instances, the employer might give you information that is useful because it allays your concerns about why you weren't selected.

For example, the employer might tell you, *For this position, we received a large number of applications, so the competition was really tough.* Then you know that for your position type, there are large numbers of applicants. If your experience is more limited, in a smaller company, or in a different industry, it's likely they were able to find candidates whose experiences matched their company's needs exactly.

You might then choose to act on that information. You might alter your job search by slightly lowering the level of position you are seeking. You could change which companies you're applying to.

If you've developed a good rapport with human resources, it's possible you can get more advice. You could say to the person on the phone, *I've applied for a few positions, and I have a couple of questions about my job search. Is there someone who I could meet with to get some advice?* Keep in mind that it won't be common for them to agree to meet with you.

However, if someone is willing to give you advice, it will be invaluable. First, it's an opportunity to show yourself as a positive, likable potential employee to a manager in human resources. If you impress that manager, you might be referred to other positions within the company or even to other companies in that industry.

It's also an opportunity to get really useful information about your job search. You might receive information and feedback you hadn't thought about. If you are lucky enough to meet with a hiring manager, be sure to follow the feedback guidelines I provide in my book *Wheels Up: Mastering the Job Interview to Launch Your Career.* In summary, don't be defensive, don't argue, and don't complain. Simply ask for advice regarding how to improve, listen, and express appreciation for the time.

Possible Reasons Why You're Not Getting An Interview

There are several possible reasons why you might not be getting an interview. If you think any of these might apply to you, adapt your job search strategies accordingly.

1. *Your expectations for the level of position you want are too high.* This could be because the experiences you have with your job title are different from the company's expectations for that same job title. A good example of this is the position of vice president in a company. In some companies a vice president role may actually be doing the duties of a lower-level director role in another company. If your title is vice president but you are not getting any interviews, you might want to start applying for director roles.

2. *Your expectations are too low relative to your experience.* The higher your level of experience and the higher your salary,

the longer it is going to take you to find a job. Therefore, if you have to move with your spouse or you're laid off, it can seem safer to keep yourself open to lower-level positions just to keep a paycheck. Generally speaking, I agree. The problem comes when your experience is so much higher than the norm for the level of position you've applied for. In those cases, the screening team may assume that you won't be happy in the lower-level position. You can combat this perception by openly addressing it in your cover letter. State the reason why you are interested in roles that are less than what would be expected for your experience. Do so in a positive way so that the employer knows you are enthusiastic about that role.

3. *You're not focused enough in your job search.* If you're keeping yourself open to a variety of job experiences, it's possible you've done so a bit *too* well. It's good to keep your options open. But you need to realize that the reason you're not getting an interview is probably because other candidates' experiences more closely match the job description. With that said, if you know you most likely won't be the best qualified candidate, apply to as many jobs as seem reasonable. You can apply with the knowledge that you have nothing to lose, and you can highlight your skills. If they want a traditional candidate, they simply won't choose you. If you are thoughtful about which positions you apply to at any one company, it doesn't hurt to try for positions that may be a stretch. However, do keep in mind the caveat in number four, below.

4. *You're applying for too many unrelated positions at one company.* If you're doing this, you'll seem desperate. If you are knowledgeably pursuing positions that are a stretch for your qualifications or skills, limit those applications to only one or two per company. In addition, keep in mind your time and your stamina. It takes a big effort to submit application paperwork. Be cautious where you spend your time. If you spend a lot of time applying for jobs that you're not really a match for, you could be tired and burned out by the time the perfect match job posting

comes your way. I think it's a better use of time to volunteer or network. This will get you more contacts than applying for multiple positions you only have a remote chance of getting.

5. *You need more connections to people who are hiring, because your job area has a very large and competitive pool of candidates.* Re-read Chapter Two for suggestions regarding how to network inside and outside your work environment.

6. *You're not being strategic about the type or size of companies you're applying to.* If you experienced a rough separation from your last position, you may need to be more strategic about the type or size of companies you're applying to. It might be obvious that you have a gap in employment. People in the industry may have heard about your job separation. If that is the case, try to apply for jobs with companies who are unlikely to care about your previous separation. Or, apply to lower level positions in order to demonstrate your acceptance that you need to hone your skills further.

7. *You need more extensive assistance from an executive coach.* As a last resort, hire a career coach or other executive coach for a one-on-one coaching session. It can get expensive, typically $200 to $500 per hour, but if you can find someone willing to coach you for an hourly rate, it might be worth it. Executive coaches can provide a wide range of services. Overall, they are a great resource to provide perspective about your approach to the job search process, given your background and experiences. They can help you analyze what weaknesses or insecurities from the past may be hindering your ability to succeed in the interview and to land the job.

Obviously, in my career I am constantly coaching others about job search and other work-life processes, so I consider myself very knowledgeable. Still, when I moved from the education industry and knew I wanted to work in the hospitality/casino world, I hired an experienced coach who works with executives at several major corporations. I wanted to get an outside perspective regarding the potential move, and I hadn't yet worked in private industry. I wasn't entirely sure if my specific skills needed to be adapted or changed to meet private industry standards.

My coach reviewed my resume, helped guide my thinking about looking for a new job, and provided support and positive thinking throughout the entire process. She also did a follow-up session after I was on the job, just to check in and be a sounding board for my new thinking and observations.

In summary, you'll probably apply to a lot of jobs without getting an interview. There will be some hits and misses. However, having read this book, you already have an advantage over the majority of candidates. You have tools in your hand to help you be both strategic and efficient when applying. And you can always email me at stacimcintosh23@gmail.com, if you have a quick question I can help provide guidance about.

Take the Shortcut

1. Try to get information from potential employers regarding the quality and clarity of the paperwork you've submitted.

2. When doing so, use strategies to get advice regarding your search in that company.

3. Get advice from the actual person hiring if you are able to do so, in order to potentially get a future referral.

4. Review the common reasons why it may be that you haven't received an interview, and adapt your job search accordingly.

5. For additional questions, feel free to email me at stacimcintosh23@gmail.com.

Chapter Nine

Need More Help?

I f you would like more extensive support for your job search via phone or in person, my husband and I own a small consulting company, Sensible Solutions. Among other resources, we provide career coaching services part-time to a limited number of individuals and groups. We work for an hourly rate outside our regular work hours, which usually means early mornings, evenings, and weekends. We also have several associates we think are fabulous and will refer you to them as well in the event our schedules are unable to accommodate your specific request. Just email me at stacimcintosh23@gmail.com if you're interested.

I also have other books providing guidance for you to succeed in every aspect of your job search and career. Check out my other books on Amazon if you want to learn more details about each aspect. Every book is short, will take you about an hour to read, and is packed with practical tips you can put into place immediately. All are published as part of the *One Hour Handbook Series.*

My other books focused on job success are currently available on Amazon in the Kindle store and in paperback form:
- *Ready for Take-Off: Preparing for Interview Questions on Your Job Search Journey*
- *Wheels Up: Mastering the Job Interview to Launch Your Career*
- Coming soon: Brace for Landing: Managing Your Life and Career After Being Laid-Off, Fired, Pushed Out or Demoted

- Coming later: *Stuck In Coach: Promotion Strategies to Land a First Class Job*

If my advice in this book helped you, please do me a favor and take a few minutes to write an Amazon book review. My commitment to readers is that I will continue to write easy to read, accessible handbooks for those who don't have the time or money to invest in expensive books, personal coaching, or on-line courses to help their career. Reader reviews help sell books, and selling books allows me the opportunity to provide more job success content to an even broader audience. Writing a review is easy to do. If you don't want to use your real name, you can easily adapt your existing Amazon account to create an anonymous Amazon public profile name. Whatever name you choose will be on the review. Reviews let other readers like you know how the book might help them. If you take the time to write a review, I will gladly put you on my mailing list to receive free advance copies of new handbooks before they are available to the public.

Chapter Ten

No Regrets

One of my most trusted mentors is a woman by the name of Barb Wright. Barb hired me into human resources without any experience, and she toogoing to use a skill list at the top of yourk the time to train me over ten years. At the heart of it, she is the reason I am able to write this book today. When she retired, I was hired to be Barb's replacement. Extremely wise, Barb always advised people to think, *Thank you for hiring me. Thank you for not hiring me.* The point was, if you give it your all and they still don't hire you, then you just aren't a match for that organization. Which means you wouldn't have been happy working there anyway. When you have no regrets about how you performed in the interview, it's easy to be at peace thinking to yourself, *It's their loss.*

My hope for you after your interview is that you have no regrets. I love to hear the experiences of my readers! Please share your "No Regrets" story by emailing me at stacimcintosh23@gmail.com or by posting your experience on my Facebook page @StaciMcIntoshBooks. Also feel free to email me if you have a question or if you want to give me suggestions for new content. You can also pay it forward and inspire others by sharing your "No Regrets" story as part of your Amazon book review. Experience is the best teacher, so I may use your story in future editions of this book!

Staci McIntosh can be contacted via the following:

Email: stacimcintosh23@gmail.com
Facebook: @McIntoshBooks
Twitter: @StaciVegas

I very much appreciate you taking the time to write an Amazon book review.

29622945R00066

Made in the USA
San Bernardino, CA
16 March 2019